4,00

I Beg To Differ

by

Frank Lowe

A Collection

Infocor Limited, Montreal

To The Women In My Life:

Hazel, Patricia, Gladys, Irene, Deanie, Anita and Lois.

Introduction

Despite what you might have heard, there is one very good thing about my column, I Beg To Differ.

I have had very little to do with it.

Anita Colby, once known as The Face, the person for whom the phrase Cover Girl was coined and at one time the world's greatest model, dreamed up the idea for the column.

At that time Anita was president of Women's News Service, a New York feature syndicate supplying copy to many of the better newspapers in the United States and Canada.

I was Anita's editor. So when she suggested we have an opinion column, written from the male point of view to balance our other output, I agreed.

The fact is, I usually agreed with Anita, And not for the customary reasons (fear of hunger, for instance) an editor may agree with his boss.

I mean, how many editors have had a boss with honey-gold hair, sea-green eyes and a figure — well, let's keep this fit for the family, eh?

So we were to have a column. But what to call it? When I was 17 I had a sports column called, The Lowe Down. Somehow I figured this kind of thing would be out-dated in New York, in 1957.

When faced with such a mammoth editorial decision in those days I knew what to do. I asked Lois Benjamin, my managing editor, what to do.

Lois, who is now Lois Gould and an ultra-with-it novelist so successful that today when I am in New York she meets me for lunch exactly 30 minutes late, said:

"Call it, I Beg To Differ."

As I always say, what separates the great editor from the average editor is a good managing editor.

Then there was the small problem of what to write about. But it occurred to me that if I was to present the male point of view of life as it is lived, I had a ready-made group of script writers.

These were Hazel, my wife; Patricia, my daughter; and (the best dead-pan commentator of them all) my mother-in-law, Deanie. For background I could draw on my memories of growing up with Gladys and Irene, my mother and sister, respectively.

Thus equipped, I sent out the first few columns. It took root in such diverse places as Boston and Miami, with way-stops at Memphis and New Orleans and about 25 other US communities.

But the column died on my return to Weekend Magazine a couple of years later. I was too busy getting my jollies covering riots and minor wars to worry about it.

I figured the whole thing had been decently buried until 1960 when the late Fred Danks, then general manager of Canada Wide Features and a nice guy who would sometimes let friendship outweigh other considerations, suggested I revive it.

Since then it has graced the editorial page of The Montreal Star every Tuesday, Thursday and Saturday, sometimes to the dismay of those who believe editorial pages should actually say something. The Sudbury Star and The Victoria Colonist, otherwise respectable journals, also carry it.

So you can see, I have had very little to do with I Beg To Differ. Except for writing it. In fact, this book which

includes some of my Weekend Magazine columns, would not have come out if it had not been for a large and intimidating type, Mike (The Big Bax) Baxendale, of Infocor, who insisted on publishing it; Paul Rush, managing editor of Weekend Magazine, who made the selection, and Max Newton, Weekend Magazine art director, who designed it.

As for me, I am merely an innocent by-stander.

F.L.
Montreal
August, 1973

Published by
Infocor Limited
Information Services Division
245 St. James Street West
Montreal

Canadian Trade Distribution by
McGraw-Hill Ryerson Limited
330 Progress Avenue
Scarborough, Ontario

ISBN 088890-011-2

Cover and design—Max Newton

Printed and bound in Canada

Contents

Part I: NOSTALGIA
>
> or Reminiscences of a boy from Bible Hill.

A boy, a brook . . . brr 13
Remember those steam whistles? 15
Those computers ruined the election 18
Useful institution may soon be gone 20
Scotch on the rocks 23
Fifty can be fun 25
The village wasn't always like that 28
Nicotine addiction and Sunday school 30
Yet another victim of progress 32
. . . And a star to steer her by 35
Portrait of a chef as a young man 37
Reunions can be disillusioning 39
Only fight with friends 41
Just nothing new under the sun 44
A sad end to a varied career 46
Of beans and booze 49
Be it never so humble 51
Loss of a dog . . . and memories 53

Part II: MY FAMILY
>
> or My mother-in-law moves in mysterious ways

My wife's a pre-worrier 59
Some things are best forgotten 61
Family trends in electioneering 63
Marital puzzle not solved 66
Love letters in the "quick sand" 68
Burglars beware 70
The rubber-tired wraith 72
Phone home for trouble 74
Perhaps we should rename labor day 76
Football ritual vs. wives 79
Whither thou goest she's going too 81
The true menace of Christmas 84
On facing up to a storm crisis 86
Crisis in the church 89
It's the wife who pays 90

Part III: MY FLOWERS

> or they never promised me a rose garden

Love me, love my yard 95
The watch on the rose 97
I can hear them giggling now 99
Be ruthless with your roses 102
Skeptics beware—the roses may hear 104

Part IV: CURRENT EVENTS

> or The media are the message

The old Canadian male 109
Speed kills 111
You can't get there from here 113
Time out for planning 115
Once seen, always forgotten 117
What is needed is more followers 119
Fashion nightmare now on the stocks 121
Intimate glimpses into the obvious 123
Statistics will kill us 126
A guided tour of the fleshpots 128
The Rolling Stones gather no praise 130
All that quiver need't be guilty 133
Brown paper bags and their uses 135
Lester Pearson: the man 137
Girls that lovely should dance a lot 139

Part V: MY WORLD

> or "You mean you get paid for just making
> that stuff up out of your head?"

Paint the town pink 145
Tales of naughty suburbs pure fiction 147
Happy discovery at a today movie 149
A haircut went to my head 151
Gloom keeps them happy 154
The face is familiar but 156
Write and wrong 158
A tip of the hat to Sinatra 160
Manifestations of affluence 162
Varying views on punctuality 165
Those games that people play 167
Distant drumming heard in the kitchen 170

Sound and fury all for naught 172
My life-long battle with the telephone 175
Time to exercise caution 177
Don't regret a thing, mom 179
Just buying a car can make you a social outcast 182
Let's leave poor Nessie alone 184
Recollections of a gunman 185
In a submarine you have to know how to use
    your head 187

Part VI: EATING AND DRINKING
          or Martinis and life's other important things

The martini (I) 193
The martini (II) 195
When summers were worth living 198
A simple song of thanksgiving 200
Breakfast can be beautiful 202
Dazzling menu for corn lovers 205
Tummies get old, too 207
Yo, ho, ho, and kindred demons 209
And all because of an aching back 212
Home-made ice cream (I) 214
Home-made ice cream (II)................. 217
A taste of the past 219
What is more cultural than home-made pie 221
The greatest put down of all 223

Part 1

NOSTALGIA

or

Reminiscences of a boy from Bible Hill

Ernest Hillen, Weekend Magazine staff writer, returned from his first assignment to the Mysterious East (Nova Scotia to the uninitiated) to report to me: "My God, Bible Hill actually exists. I thought you had invented it."

A boy, a brook ... brr

The first really sunny and warm day of spring invariably finds me up to my hocks in nostalgia and feeling terribly sorry for all kids who today have to spend the first real day of spring in the city.

Sure, I know today's urban kids have parks and playgrounds and streets. And they would probably be horrified to have to welcome spring as I did — a hayseed who grew up in a small suburb of a small town.

But for quite a few years in this tiny place the first warm spring day, if it fell on a Saturday, got an appropriate greeting. A bunch of us would get together in the morning and head for the railway track leading from Nova Scotia to Upper Canada.

Any freight going west at this point had to slow down for the slight, but very long grade. So it was a simple matter to swing aboard and ride for several miles, courtesy of the CNR.

Mind you, we had to know the precise moment the freight reached the top of the grade. Because after that it was a downhill run and any kid who didn't jump just as the freight was moving over the top of the grade was going to get a fast ride to Amherst. And a homecoming which would make sitting down uncomfortable for about a week.

Anyway, at the top of the grade we all would jump. We would be only about three miles from home, but in that area being three miles out of town was the equivalent of being 103 miles out of today's cities.

There was nothing but woods — and a brook.

The brook, of course, was the reason for our trek. There was a river running right through our suburb, but this river was always in full view of the adults. Spring could not be properly and ceremoniously greeted there — not with all those nosy adults around.

After we walked down from the railway track, through a copse and came to our brook, we would all stretch out in the sun. The ground was probably a little damp and cold but we ignored this and concentrated on telling each other how wonderful the sun felt, how warm it was.

Then, as inevitably as in any ritual devised by primitive people to welcome the sun back, one of the gang would get up and peer at the brook, running deep and fast and black as it carried the spring run-off down to Cobequid Bay. In the summer this brook was a lazy trickle. But in April it was a tiger of a stream, fat and turbulent and noisy.

"Last one across is a rotten egg," this gang member would say, starting to take off his clothes. And the rest of us would cluster on the bank and look at the foam-topped flood waters and shiver with delightful apprehension.

One boy would always mention that he wasn't allowed to go swimming in April.

Another, usually a newcomer to the group, would mention the possibility of drowning in that awesome, all-of-20-foot-wide sluice of flood water. This would be hooted down by fellows who, well primed on Boys' Own Annual and Chums, made retorts such as "Ya wanna live forever?" But the prospect of drowning was probably the exciting and enticing reason all of us were girding ourselves to jump into the brook.

After all, it was spring, wasn't it? And a fellow had to do something, something exciting, to welcome spring, didn't he?

Even now, as I look out of my office window at the first

14

real spring sun, I can recall the agonizing moment when that spring water closed over my head. The breath squeezed out of my body by the cold. The rushing water tumbling me down the channel as I thrashed to the surface.

Then there was the wonder of actually climbing ashore. Once again I had not only welcomed spring. I had survived it. The walk in the sun felt good as I set out for the little footbridge that would take me over the stream — no, we never swam back, for heavens sake — to where my clothes were.

Our little pagan ritual was over. And spring was officially in.

April 15, 1967.

Remember those steam whistles?

Frankly, I have never had any desire to be prime minister. We Canadians have a tendency to treat our prime ministers rather roughly, and I don't think my blood pressure could take such treatment.

But every so often, I must admit, the prime minister's office does seem to have some advantages. The other day, for instance, Prime Minister Trudeau had the opportunity to drive an old-fashioned steam engine.

Not only that, he was allowed to yank the cord to unleash that wonderful, eerie sound of the almost forgotten steam whistle.

The sound of that whistle — the long, echoing, lonesome wail — was once as much a Canadian symbol as the beaver or maple leaf. Perhaps even more so.

The whistle of the steam engine to many a Canadian boy and girl meant escape, romance, adventure.

It has all but disappeared from the land now, but everybody of a certain age must know what I am talking about. And the fog-horn-like noise made by the modern diesel will never replace those memories.

For thousands of kids, living in small towns and villages along the steel strips that held Canada together, this steam whistle was a promise.

A promise that some day we would be able to get out of those small towns and villages — and a guarantee that we were not completely isolated.

In my home town, where two trans-Canada passenger trains stopped each day, you could even distinguish the engineers by the sound of the whistle.

When one particular engineer, for instance, was in charge of the morning train I could lie in bed and anticipate what was going to happen.

When his great engine crested the hill back of the town he would pull down the cord. Now, I realize that the whistle was supposed to be used to warn when the train was approaching a level crossing, but he forgot that when he was high-balling for home.

The first sound would be a few short, joyous yips. Then, as the express plunged down the incline, the sound would change to a series of long, wailing blasts that echoed out over the marsh and seemed to hang in the air for minutes after the whistle had stopped blowing.

For a small boy, lying in the dark in his bedroom at the back of the house, this was all very reassuring. The express was still running and those haunting, mournful sounds filling the pre-dawn air assured me that some day I too would be on that train to somewhere.

Later, when I did start moving around a bit, I found that the steam locomotive whistle was not merely the property of my home town. I hated to admit it, but the sound was even more stirring, more nostalgia-making out on the prairie.

Naturally, a kid or even a young man does not go around telling people he is in love with a steam locomotive whistle. So I never talked about this peculiarity of mine.

At least, I thought it was a peculiarity until I went overseas. Then, towards the end of the war and at a time when many of the Canadians there had been away from home for quite a few years, I found I was not alone.

The CBC International Service instituted a program for the troops overseas. Its introduction was that symbol of the Canada of those days — a long, nostalgic blast of a steam locomotive whistle.

I swear that many an eye misted over a bit when this sound filled the air.

Now, I know that this sound will never return and I am not sitting here knocking the diesel engine and its peculiar-sounding horn.

But when I read where our prime minister had not only driven an old-fashioned steam locomotive, but actually had the opportunity to once more let loose the haunting sound of a steam locomotive whistle, I simply had to get rid of my envy some way.

And my nostalgia.

July 4, 1970.

Those computers ruined the election

Damn the computers. I mean, here we have just lived through a rouser of an election, a cliffhanger, a hair-raiser. And half the fun of watching is taken from us because of those damned computers.

In the old days watching a good, close, country-wide election unfold was an unrivalled sport. Each viewer was his own expert, and when a roomful of viewers got together the mayhem was great.

The Eastern Seaboard states got things started. As every Canadian figures these states, and political figures are all part of his own backyard, there isn't too much tension there.

It is a time to get the pretzels out, make sure there is enough beer in the refrigerator and generally limber up for the main bout.

Things begin to hot up as the first returns trickle in from those more exotic states in the midwest. This is when the election began to live up to its tradition of being a great participation sport.

If a two percent return showed on the election board one expert could turn to another expert in the living room and say:

"Well, I guess that wraps it up. I have an aunt living at Pollsters Crik and she wrote only a week ago to tell me it would be a Democratic sweep in that state."

But the other expert wasn't going to take that without an argument. No sir.

"Your aunt my eye," he would say. "Why, I was actually there not more than a month ago. Spent two days in Otter City. And I know that is Republican country, son. You just wait and see."

That's the way it would go on merrily all night long. Full of beer and pretzels and opinions, the viewers had a wonderful time keeping their own scores, making their projections and predictions.

But not any more.

The marathon election we just lived through is a good example of what I am talking about. At one point, for instance, two percent of a crucial state vote was shown on the board and I was all set to give my views on the matter.

I was going to tell my fellow viewers that this two percent meant nothing at all. "I travelled through that state by train a few years ago," I was going to pontificate, "and let me tell you, that state is solidly Republican."

But before I could say this the computer took over and with only two percent of the vote in conceded the state to the Democrats, for heavens sake.

It isn't that I am jealous of these computers. After all, how can one be jealous of a hunk of tin and a set of whirring wheels?

But they do have a nasty habit of putting one down.

They dehumanize the whole business of elections. In the old days, for instance, electoral battles were conceded by human beings, not metal boxes.

In those days, on election night, the newspapers set up election desks. Reporters and deskmen who could add were given charts and graphs, while those who couldn't add were sent to the polls to phone in results.

It was a great game seeing who could concede the most candidates first. One editor I knew was unrivalled in this respect — he could sense a trend even before a single ballot box had been stolen, or stuffed.

Sometimes, of course, in his rush to get the election over with so he could adjourn to more congenial surroundings than the arid newsroom, he moved a little too quickly.

There was one election, I recall, when the great man peered at a list of election results and told me to phone a prominent candidate. "Tell him we want his concession statement," he said.

I phoned. The candidate was somewhat amazed as up until then he had thought he was ahead. But, who was he to argue with our expert? So he reluctantly dictated a statement.

It was quite a few hours later, as we held an election post-mortem, that we learned our editor had erred. He had been totting up the wrong column of figures.

The editor thought about this for a moment, then said: "Oh well, he wouldn't have made a very good member anyway."

As I said, those were the days when elections were fun.

Nov. 7, 1968.

Useful institution soon may be gone

It never occurred to me just how drastically this world has changed — particularly for young adults — until I read that pawnshops were going out of business. There simply wasn't enough trade, the news item said, to keep the good, old-fashioned pawnshop going.

Now, I was dimly aware that young adults had adopted some different lifestyles. They were, or so I heard, drinking less and smoking more. In other words, there was a new kind of high in the land.

But it never occurred to me that the time would ever come when a young adult would not be in need of a quick buck a day or so prior to pay day.

And that was where your old-fashioned pawnshop played such a useful role.

Perhaps things are so changed that young people now never run short of cash. But in my day "the shorts" was a disease that afflicted almost all of us. It would be a Wednesday, you had a date that night, but you did not have any money.

It wouldn't do to attempt to borrow from a friend. Because he had tried to touch you for a deuce the day before. So you ambled over to your favorite pawnshop and hocked your watch.

Mind you, this system did have its minor risks. There was the time, for instance, when a pawnshop in which my watch was resting got hit by a bomb. My sole bit of collateral went up in a cloud of flame and masonry and dust.

My financial equilibrium was not restored until my company gave me a portable typewriter in the hope that this would inspire me to do some work when I was on out-of-town assignments.

When my stint with that outfit was over and I had to return the typewriter the boss was most impressed. "You certainly took good care of it," he said, looking at the portable.

I was too modest to tell him the truth — that, actually, I hadn't been looking after that machine. Instead, it had been resting quietly in a pawnshop for most of the time I had it.

After all, any reporter on the road who can't borrow the use of a typewriter really isn't trying.

21

I was not alone in my affection for honest pawnshops. Most of my friends were engaged in the same love affair. One I know of — I won't mention his name because he is now a respectable editorial writer — once inherited a large accordion.

Fortunately for the state of our friendship, he never tried to learn to play the thing. But time and again it saved us from all those ugly side-effects usually associated with malnutrition.

There were also those plutocrats, a kind of aristocracy of the plebians. If there can be such a thing. These were young men who had inherited a little something from a relative. Not money, naturally. But something like a good diamond ring. Or a genuine pearl stick-pin.

These young men had no use for such accessories as far as wearing apparel went. But they were given the red carpet treatment in the pawnshop of their choice when they decided that it was time to raise a bit of scratch via the family heirloom route.

The pawnshop, in fact, was a way of life. Today, for heaven's sake, people actually *pay* to have their winter coats stored through the summer. Then, we took our coats to the pawnshop where they were not only looked after all summer — we actually had a little money to spend in those first gay, carefree days of spring.

However now, or so I am told, many old and honorable pawnshops are quietly fading away. Their once indispensable services are no longer needed, it would seem.

Today, I guess, everybody is so affluent no one even recalls that that old song, Pop Goes The Weasel, was once the national anthem for those of us who used the pawnshops regularly. Or that the term to "pop the weasel" meant to put something into hock.

Sic transit penury.

Scotch on the rocks

Each time one of these Royal visits take place I get all excited. Mainly because I hope that this will be the occasion for the Duke of Edinburgh to pay back the bottle of Scotch he owes me.

Mind you, when the visit ends and I still have failed to receive the bottle, I'm really not annoyed. After all, he's pretty busy during these Royal clambakes and it would sound a little silly if he said he had to disappear for an hour or so to pay off a debt.

The debt was incurred quite a few years ago. Prince Philip was making a tour of the Canadian Arctic and I was one of the reporters assigned to follow him. All went without incident until the Royal party, and the press, holed up at an outpost at the tip of Great Bear Lake, within spitting distance of the Arctic Circle.

That night, as sleeping accommodations were not too plentiful in that area, I decided to sleep in the plane. It must have been about 5 a.m. when I woke up, and discovered one of the ropes holding our old Canso amphibian in place had worked loose.

So I immediately edged out onto the wing to attempt to remedy this. And promptly fell into Great Bear Lake — not one of Canada's highly recommended swimming spas.

When I reached shore, soaked and colder than any human has a right to be, I was amazed to be greeted by one of the Duke's entourage. While I stood there with my heavy flannels dripping water, he stood immaculate in full morning dress. At first I figured the shock of falling into that ice water had snapped my mental moorings.

"Do you always go for a morning swim?" he asked.

I assured him this was not the case, especially when the water was about 33 degrees, give or take a degree.

"My good man," he then said, "you'd better get into some dry clothes. And a good strong drink — that would help."

I was so perishing cold I failed to detect the sneakiness of this approach. Liquor, that deep in our northland, is a scarce and valuable commodity. Anyone who has any is a natural dupe for the born con man.

But, without a thought in my mind but to get out of those wet clothes and into a glass of Scotch (and thank you, Mr. Benchley) I grabbed a nearby boat and rowed myself and the Prince's aide out to the Canso.

He was most solicitous. He helped me out of my sopping clothes, helped me dry myself and even reminded me about the therapeutic qualities of Scotch at such times.

Still without a suspicious thought in that cavity I call my mind, I delved deep into my duffle bag. There, camouflaged against scroungers in layers of long underwear and woollen shirts, reposed my last bottle of Scotch.

I poured a noggin into a tin cup. It warmed me all the way to my toes. Then, remembering my manners, I poured another noggin for myself, and one for my unexpected guest.

"Delicious," he said, smacking his lips. "Just what the Prince might need."

"Not this he won't," I said, clutching the last bottle of Scotch within a radius of at least 1,000 miles. "Not this."

"Come now," the aide said. "I'm in a terrible spot. Through some oversight the Royal Party is out of Scotch. And if the Prince wants a drink today, and I can't give him one, he could become very angry."

I looked at my bottle of Scotch. I considered my loyalties. Then I looked at the aide — he was well over six feet tall and there I was, five-foot-six of solid flab alone with him at 5 a.m. in a beat-up Canso somewhere on Great Bear Lake. I didn't have a chance.

"Well," I said, with something close to a sob in my voice. "Let's have one for the road, just the two of us, and then, well, then you can take the bottle to the Prince."

"You'll never regret it, old chap," the aide said. "I'll see that the Prince repays you."

With that he and my bottle disappeared.

As I said, that was almost 12 years ago. Since then the Prince has come and gone quite a few times. But I am still short one bottle of Scotch.

You know, sometimes I have the feeling that that aide never really told the Prince whose bottle he was drinking out of up there at Great Bear Lake. Do you suppose that is the answer?

July 4, 1967.

Fifty can be fun

Fourteen years ago I went to a lot of trouble and flew a lot of miles simply to attend a friend's 50th birthday.

Frankly, it wasn't all that much fun. My friend, when I met him, was glum, to say the least. It seems that his birthday had started when his boss congratulated him on receiving a raise.

"A raise?" my friend queried happily. "I didn't know I was getting a raise."

"Don't you read the newspapers?" the boss enquired. "The old age pension has just been increased."

Somehow, my friend did not think this was very funny.

After the alleged party, my friend and I were standing together waiting for a cab. And he sighed and said:

"You know, now that I am 50 I realize that I am everything I despised when I was 21."

I thought about that particular occasion quite a bit this recent April Fool's Day. Because on April Fool's Day I, too, marked my 50th birthday. (After all, on what more appropriate day could I be born?)

Anyway, after quite a bit of thought, and just before I said to hell with it, and went to sleep, it occurred to me that my friend had been unduly shook up about that traumatic 50 mark.

Now, I guess, the real horror when it comes to birthdays is the 30-year mark. I mean, after 30 you are dead. One girl I know actually told me that when she reached 30 she was going to go skiing — and find a cliff to plunge over.

Somehow, I doubt if she will actually do this.

Fortunately, I grew up in an age when such horrors — or anticipated horrors — were unknown. And come to think of it, I am finding there is not anything particularly horrible about the number 50, either.

In fact, when I was remembering my friend's gloomy comparison between being 21 and 50, I came to the conclusion that perhaps he was exaggerating.

This doesn't mean I was unhappy when I was 21. Far from it.

I was doing what I wanted to do — reporting. Also, I was able to indulge my second love by being a sea-going reporter. The one disturbing factor, I suppose, was that I was a sea-going reporter because there was a war and those Atlantic cruises were not all that pleasurable.

Sometimes, I remember, they could be downright dicey.

But one good thing about them was that they prevented one from brooding about the future.

Mainly because it was quite conceivable that there would be no future.

My 21st birthday was a good one, as I recall. I spent most of that day on a troop ship and when I stepped ashore I had to file a story.

My editor's birthday gift was my first major byline — the best birthday gift I ever received.

Then, of course, the local friendly bootlegger arrived just before midnight delivering that good, black Demerara rum in milk bottles painted white on the inside so a casual observer might actually think he was delivering milk.

A few phone calls did the rest.

The only one who didn't appreciate it was the boss. The next morning he looked at his somewhat wilted junior reporter, pointed at the usually glossy surface of his desk and opined:

'If you had to have girls dance on my desk I think it was most thoughtful of you to have them dance in their bare feet — I wouldn't want my desk scratched."

I waited for the axe to fall, but he merely added: "Oh yes, a belated happy birthday."

As I said, it was fun to be 21. But I would hate to be so tied to nostalgia that I thought that was the only age to be.

It really isn't you know. Fifty has a lot going for it, too.

April 3, 1971.

The village wasn't always like that

The article was about today's Greenwich Village in New York. And it read like this:

"Now only the very desperate or the very hardened choose to live in the neighborhood . . . a land of heroin, commonplace violence and cheap wine."

Somehow that made me feel very sad. Because there was a time, not all that long ago, when to be young and to live in the Village was one of the nicest combinations that could happen to a person.

I know, because I was there. My tiny home was on 10th Street. At the bottom of the street there was a place called Nick's and on a Sunday afternoon, for the price of a cold beer, one could sit and listen to the greats of the jazz world jamming away in impromptu pick-up groups.

Desperation and violence were never a part of that scene, or any other scene that I can recall. In fact, we never thought of such possibilities and on warm spring nights a guy and his girl could stroll those crazy, winding streets in the dark without a worry.

It never occurred to me that I should be careful about where I ambled, or that I should worry about what might happen if I dropped into a strange place. There were always people to meet and music to listen to and stories to swap.

Nobody had much money, of course, but nobody seemed to need much money. When I wanted to splurge, I could take a girl to any one of a dozen small but cosy restaurants where, for $2.50 each, we could consume a four-course meal.

Drinks were 35 cents each and on a Saturday night a violinist would roam around the tables. Schmaltzy, but fun.

Most of the time we weren't that formal. I was at that time an overnight editor, which meant I had to get to work at midnight. So it was up at about 6 p.m., and breakfast in the little Mexican place in the basement of my apartment house.

Chili for breakfast? Well, if that didn't appeal I could walk across the small square and start the day with spaghetti and meatballs — 35 cents.

After that anything might happen. About 9 p.m., for instance, Marie at the Crisis Bar would be warming up the piano for the night. Or somebody might invite me to join a group where we would talk about the novels we were going to write and the plays we were going to produce.

Strangely enough, a few of those people actually did go on to do just that. But then that wasn't important. What was important was to be together and *know* we were going to do it.

When I got out of the office in the morning it was great to amble along in the sun and realize that while most other people were cooped up at work, I had the day ahead of me and nothing to do except what I wanted to do.

A walk down to the river if it was a nice day? Fine. Perhaps, if it was raining, a cup of coffee and a book in a snug café?

In my youthful ignorance and euphoria it seemed to me that this kind of life might last forever. In fact, I remember once a group of us talked about that far-off day when we would be old (we really didn't believe this would really happen, of course) and what we would do then.

My response was that I would retire and live in the Village. Each day about 10 a.m. I would stroll out, buy a copy of the New York Times, then sit at a sidewalk table and read and eat.

However, from what I read and what I hear, I guess I will have to change my retirement plans. The kind of Village I remember doesn't exist any more.

Sept. 9, 1971.

Nicotine addiction and Sunday school

Sometimes as I listen to the present brouhaha about the pros and cons of the government plan to ban cigarette advertising, I wonder just how this will affect the incidence of people who decide to take up the weed.

I mean, do those glossy advertisements really persuade young people to take up smoking?

Lacking a competent research staff to answer that question, I have to depend on my childhood memories.

As I recall it, the whole thing started because I went to Sunday School.

One day a group of us was reluctantly treading the longest and most round-about route to the Sunday School, and as usual we were talking about how lucky our Roman Catholic friends were.

They went to church in the morning and then had the afternoon free. We benighted WASPs went to church in the morning and then, at 3 p.m., went back for an hour-long spiritual bath known as Sunday School.

30

This effectively ruined our Sunday afternoons, or so we felt.

This particular day, after we had exhausted this subject and had given up trying to think of ways to persuade our parents to switch religious allegiances, we performed our weekly ritual.

All of us carried a church envelope. The single envelope was divided into two separate containers. In one was a nickel for the upkeep of the Sunday School. In the other was a nickel for the upkeep of foreign missions.

None of us thought very highly of foreign missions. Mainly because about once a month one of these missionaries would turn up at the Sunday School and, after we had already spent an hour there, would take up an additional hour telling us about their work with the heathen.

So, to get even and to bolster our spending money, each of us would use a razor to slit the bottom of the foreign mission section of the envelope and retrieve the nickel therein.

Usually we bought candy with this windfall. But on this occasion I stepped up to the counter of the corner candy store, plunked down my nickel and said:

"A package of Turrets, please."

In those days a package of five Turrets cost exactly five cents.

Why did I do such an awful thing? Had I come across some particularly seductive bit of cigarette advertising?

Frankly, I don't think so. But what had gotten to me were those sophisticated kids in Grade 8 — the highest grade in the school I attended at the time — who strolled languidly out at the end of the day and lit up once they were off the school grounds.

That was real class. And what a 13-year-old could do, a six-year-old could do, too. Hence the sudden decision to buy a pack of Turrets rather than a gooey, gorgeous Sweet

Marie chocolate bar.

That particular hour of Sunday School seemed longer and more tedious than usual. Then, to cap it all, a lady from a mission in what was then known as Formosa came, with endless color slides and a projector, to tell us how our mission was doing there.

But finally we were turned loose. We headed at a dead run for the bushes around the river bank where, safe from prying eyes, we could try out the magic of smoking.

We were already visualizing how startled those sophisticates in Grade 8 would be when, come Monday, we too lit up on our walk home.

Well, it didn't exactly work out that way. I might have been ready and eager to smoke. But my stomach wasn't.

Yet that is how it all began.

Sept. 21, 1971.

Yet another victim of progress

The brass key is dead.

This bald, brief statement is liable to bring a bored "so what?" from many older people, and a "what's a brass key?" reaction from the younger set.

But to some of us who grew up in the business which now is stylishly referred to as "communications," the brass key was the bedrock of our existence. And the people who pounded the brass key were a grand and diverse breed of individuals.

To clear up the confusion, the brass key, of course, is the little machine used to transmit Morse code messages. Or, it *was* used to transmit Morse code messages.

Today these machines are silent. The last Morse code message in Canada was tapped out two days ago, and "communications" became the property of such cold and unknowable machines as the telex and the microwave.

When I was a boy the brass key was the world's greatest toy. First, one had to learn the Morse code—the dots and dashes symbolizing various letters of the alphabet.

Then came long, voluntary sessions with the text books until one got to the point where one could build sending and receiving sets.

I can remember being in my bedroom when my home-made receiver would start to chatter. I would dash to my key and knock out a reply.

The fact that I was talking to the kid next door, with whom I had been talking person-to-person all day, did not diminish the thrill.

Here we were, linked up by a precariously strung wire, in constant contact through the mysterious dot-dash-dot of a brass key.

One reason why I wasn't overly excited about man reaching the moon, perhaps, was that I had already lived through that ultimate scientific experience — the fact that two kids, with the help of some know-how, wire and a couple of brass keys, could communicate with each other at any time.

Later, as a very young reporter, that brass key played an even more important role in my life. In my part of the world exciting news stories generally happened in fairly inaccessible places. Telephones, to get the news back to the office, were rare and not too reliable.

But somewhere, at some rail depot, there was bound to be a man with an eye shade hunched over a brass key. If I could get to him, he would get the news through.

These brass pounders were a tough and independent lot. They were by nature drifters — their knowledge guaranteed them jobs wherever they might go.

So if they didn't like your looks, or your approach, they would simply refuse to do business with you.

I remember one distinctly. I had been covering a ship wreck. After I got the story I headed for a small community where I knew there was a Morse key.

When I got there and explained the problem, the operator shrugged and said, "Sorry — I gotta send the fish reports."

After the fish reports had gone it seems he had to send the weather report. My story was quietly rotting in my hot little hands.

Finally, for the first time, he looked at me. "Why didn't you tell me you were Howard Lowe's son?" he asked crossly.

Then, wasting no more time in such useless conversation as explaining how he knew my late father (I discovered he had sailed as a Morse operator in one of my father's ships), he sent my priceless prose on to the head office.

Brass pounders were also good news sources. These men did not feel that operating the key was a chore — they loved doing it. So when official business wasn't being cleared, they would gossip up and down the wire.

A young reporter in search of news only had to form a working relationship with a brass pounder to find out what was happening for miles around. Fires, floods, births, deaths — and the latest dirty jokes. They all came clattering out of the Morse key.

It was a homey, human kind of operation. For one, I will miss it.

June 1, 1972.

... And a star to steer her by

The news story read like this: "Gulf Canada's mammoth tanker, the 326,562 deadweight ton Universe Japan, called at Point Tupper, N.S. It is the largest ship to cross the Atlantic to dock at a Western hemisphere port . . ."

And all I can say is that I bet on this historic occasion the skipper of the Universe Japan was not nearly as elated as was Capt. Lowe, age nine, when he sailed his first command through those same waters.

Mind you, my ship was not the largest by any means. It was, in fact, the ferry that then carried people and cars and trains from mainland Nova Scotia to Cape Breton.

Since then a causeway has been built to span the strait so I presume the ferries are no longer needed.

But back when I was nine they were in operation. So one summer, when visiting a friend in Mulgrave, I began to haunt the docks of that small, Nova Scotia port.

The fishing boats were fun and occasionally a kid could hitch a ride in one of them. But the monsters in the port were the car ferries — well, they were monsters in my eyes.

It took a little doing, but eventually I got to know the skipper of one of these ships. He was a kindly man so he allowed me to stand on the bridge with him as he travelled back and forth.

He taught me to box the compass and explained about port and starboard and red lights and green lights and the proper names for various parts of the ship.

To me, this was a floating Nirvana.

Then, just a day or so before I was going to have to say goodbye and return to my landlubberly ways, he said casually at the start of one trip:

"How about taking her across?"

At first I was stunned. Surely he wasn't going to let me take this monstrous, wonderful craft across all that water — a whole mile of it, at least?

When it sank in that he did mean it, I was panic-stricken. All those people, all this equipment, dependent on me.

Now you know and I know now that there was absolutely no danger. I would be allowed to hold the wheel, with the regular quartermaster at my elbow, and turn it to the captain's commands.

But then, as I clutched the spokes of the great wheel — and tried to see by looking around it as I couldn't see over it — well, life doesn't hand out too many thrills of that nature, let me tell you.

Perhaps if today I won a Nobel prize for literature I might once again approximate how I felt way back then. But somehow I doubt it.

For most of that glorious day I piloted the ferry between Mulgrave and Port Hawkesbury, always remembering to "let 'er slide a little" coming up to nearby Point Tupper to compensate for the constant five-knot tide.

I never once bumped a piling or scraped a side, I'll have you know. And when I got to my friend's place for supper I was so tired I could hardly consume more than two pieces of pie.

I had been clutching that wheel so tightly — I didn't dare let go when the ship was quietly tied up loading her next cargo — my hands and arms ached.

To cap it all my host and father of my friend, Dr. Breen, never cracked a smile as I told him of the worries and responsibilities of being in command.

In fact, Dr. Breen, an enthusiastic amateur sailor, merely nodded when I commented: "I guess small sail boats are all right, but to really find out what it is all about you have to take over a large steamship."

As I said, it was a day and an occasion to remember. So when I read that news item about the arrival of the Universe Japan in my old waters, I realized that her skipper must have been proud of his record-setting achievement.

But not as proud as I was that day I was in charge of the car ferry.

April 4, 1972.

Portrait of a chef as a young man

Each Christmas day as I gorge myself with the traditional turkey I silently give thanks that I am married — and no longer have to face up to preparing a turkey myself.

Because there was a Christmas when I and a batch of unsuspecting friends sat down to a turkey dinner that I had prepared. And let me tell you, memories such as that stay with a fellow for a long, long time.

It was a wartime Christmas in London. There was a scarcity of everything, particularly turkeys.

But the butcher where I regularly exchanged my ration coupons decided that I should have a turkey. I tried to argue with him, but it was no use. He had a turkey for me, and it would be very rude of me to refuse it.

37

For two days prior to Christmas I read a cook book, flamboyantly titled "What Every Bride Should Know." It made the whole operation sound so ridiculously simple that I invited a group of friends for Christmas dinner.

"It will be just like home," I told them, full of misplaced confidence. "Turkey and all the trimmings."

The first part of the Christmas party was a great success. The girl who later became my wife had seen to it that there was plenty of cheer.

Way back in Canada she had bought herself a small soldering set from Woolworth's. She would then go out and buy up cans of tomato juice.

After the tomato juice was poured down the sink and the cans washed inside, she would re-fill them with good Canadian booze. The soldering set closed up the punctures and not even the sharpest-eyed customs man, or greediest longshoreman, would suspect that these cans shipped to a Canadian in wartime London contained not tomato juice, but grade-A Scotch.

So, as I said, the first part of the Christmas party went along very well.

Perhaps it went so well that I forgot to look at the turkey in the oven after the first few peeks. Or maybe I forgot about the time.

But eventually somebody announced that it was eight o'clock, and wondered when we were going to enjoy that "turkey and all the trimmings."

"Any moment now," I replied nonchalantly, making my way out to the kitchen. The "trimmings" had come from Canada in cans, and merely had to be heated.

As this heating process was going on, I opened the oven and looked at my bird. It was stone cold dead in the oven.

Whoever had written "What Every Bride Should Know" had forgotten one very important instruction.

Such as: "After placing turkey in oven, remember to turn on oven, Dum-dum."

I must say, perhaps thanks to the plethora of converted tomato cans in my apartment, the guests took the delay with fairly good grace.

In fact, any unsuspecting outsider might have thought that all Canadians ate Christmas dinner about 2 a.m. on Boxing Day.

And nobody complained about the turkey. In fact, a few days later when I worked up my courage to the point where I could ask one of my friends what he had thought of my turkey, he replied:

"Turkey? What turkey?"

But he was very enthusiastic about my brand of Scotch.

Dec. 29, 1969.

Reunions can be disillusioning

It was with real glee that I received a nice phone call recently, inviting me to a reunion of a group of people I had once been involved with some 25 years ago — we had all more or less worked together in a common endeavor to prolong the war.

Now, I haven't told anyone this before, but the fact that I had never been invited to a reunion of any kind was beginning to give me an inferiority complex. Friends of mine were always sprinting away to attend class reunions, old home weeks and such things.

But I never went anywhere. I was beginning to suspect

that perhaps no one who had ever met me wanted to admit the fact.

Then came this invitation. And let me tell you, if I had an inferiority complex before the reunion, after the reunion I replaced it with a completely shattered ego.

At first all went well. Then I spotted a fellow I had once shared combat with — if 19 pubs in one night doesn't qualify as combat I don't know what does — and dashed over to say hello. He looked puzzled for a moment. Then he cried:

"Why Frank Lowe — I didn't know you. You've put on so much weight . . ."

After that I was a lot more careful and finally manoeuvred close to a fellow who had the same manly contours. He was a guy named Ted, a real knucklehead as I remember him. The kind of fellow who gives morons a bad name.

And within 30 seconds I learned he now is vice-president of a huge corporation, lives in a $75,000 home and smokes nothing but $2 cigars.

Finally he paused and, dribbling cigar ash down the front of my one good suit, asked: "What are you doing — still pounding a typewriter?"

A neighbor of his chimed in. "That's what I tell my kid — writing is okay as a hobby so long as a fellow has a good, steady job."

An older man, a guy who once wore red tabs and tried to explain the mysteries of map reading to me, came over. For a little while I basked in the warmth of his kindly reminisences. Then he asked what I was doing these days. I said I was working for a newspaper. He said:

"What a pity, and your mother had such high hopes for you."

By this time I was headed in a state of complete rout for the nearest exit. But before I could reach it I barged into another former colleague. We chatted about mutual acquaintances for some time (all of whom are doing much better than yours truly, it seems) when he said:

"How's your lovely wife?"

I told him she was just fine thanks and he continued:

"In most cases a wife is referred to as a man's better half. But in your case I guess we'd have to call your wife your better nine-tenths."

When I finally got a cab I puzzled all the way home about that line. I knew he had complimented my wife. But was that all he had meant?

As a matter of fact, I guess it is best not to wonder about such things. Or anything else that happens at a jolly old reunion, at least as far as I am concerned.

Mar. 19, 1968.

Only fight with friends

There I was reading another of those articles about how tough it is to grow up today when it occurred to me that it was 30 years ago when I personally experienced a few difficulties with this growing up bit.

I checked the calendar. Sure enough, it was the first Saturday in August. And in 1938, on the first Saturday in August, I got the message that from that moment I was on my own.

It was my first weekend of being a working stiff. There I was, a long way from home, in a coal-mining town. And

I was a pretty lucky guy. After all, I had just turned 17 and I had a job that paid $8 a week.

Mind you, my room-and-board cost $6 a week. But that still left me $2 a week to throw around foolishly. And in those days there weren't many 17-year-olds who could live like that.

The town was Endsville, of course, unless you were crazy about mountains of coal slag and living in a community made up mostly of identical company houses tethered precariously to the side of a steep hill.

But I did have a job. And it was Saturday night and I had $2 in my pocket.

My landlord, a nice old guy who liked reading the newspapers but often read them upside down unless there was a picture on the page to guide him, told me "all the boys goes to the Miners' Hall" on Saturday nights.

So I went to the Miners' Hall. There was a bit of a hush when I entered. I was dressed in my best — blue blazer with brass buttons, a rather vigorous regimental tie (courtesy of an uncle), ice-cream flannels and two-tone black-and-white shoes.

The young miners were dressed in clean dark shirts, rolled to show their muscular forearms. And they wore pants. But not ice-cream flannels.

However, I was a cocky kid so when the music began I strode across the floor to the row of girls along the far wall, picked my target and said:

"May I have the pleasure?"

The kid laughed so hard you could hardly hear the fiddle. She kept doubling up, holding her middle, and between spells of laughter pointed at me and gasped:

"Did you hear that? He said, 'May I. . . .' "

But she could never finish. A new wave of hysteria would always come along to interrupt.

Somewhat disconcerted, I retreated to the wall along

42

which the males were lined. After an hour of lonely watching, I was ready to leave when a young miner came up and said: "Come on, pal — we'll go out in the park and have a drink."

The park was a greensward dotted with memorial stones — one commemorated the mine disaster of 1878 when 105 died. Another commemorated the mine disaster of 1901 when 202 died. And so on.

It wasn't a very cheery place.

The young miner handed me a bottle so I took a swig. After one gulp, if I had had any vocal cords left, I would have screamed, "I've gone blind."

But I hadn't gone blind. It was merely that the home-brew had jolted me to the point where my eye-balls had turned completely around. I had Orphan Annie eyes for about five minutes.

When my sight returned and I was persuaded to take my sophomore belt, the young miner clapped me on the back and said:

"Okay — now, do you want to hit me first, or will I hit you first? You're the guest, so you have the choice."

I tried to explain that I didn't want to hit or be hit. But he insisted that at some point during every Saturday night dance the fellows enjoyed themselves by fighting.

"We only fight with friends," he told me. "And you looked like a nice friendly fellow so I thought I'd ask you."

The rest of the evening is a bit of blur. Between belting the home-brew and being belted I kind of lost track.

It was a great introduction to adulthood. After that, nothing could really jar me.

Aug. 6, 1968.

Just nothing new under the sun

Everybody these days seems to be excited about sex education — should it be taught in the schools, or would such goings-on lead to orgies at recess time?

Frankly, I have no answer to this burning question. But it seems to me that sex education, of a sort, has been going on in schools for quite some time.

I remember, way back when, that great moment when I was entering high school. Due to a couple of teachers who wanted to get rid of me, I had been jumped several grades in grammar school, so arrived at the high school about two years younger than most new-comers.

This, plus the fact that my sister had lost a year to breaking a couple of ankles — one after the other — skiing, I arrived in high school while she was still there.

My sex education started even before the high school doors opened for my first term. For the occasion I had gone downtown and bought myself a snappy outfit.

My sister took one look at me in my new finery and screamed:

"Take those things off. It's bad enough to have a kid brother in the same school, but you are not to wear plus fours."

Lesson No. 1: plus fours are not sexy.

Then, of course, there came the problem of school dances. While my main ambition was to make the hockey team — an unlikely event with my two-year disadvantage — I also wanted to attend the dances.

Lesson No. 2: generally speaking, girls smell nicer than hockey players.

My sister decided that if I was going to go to the dances, at least I should learn to dance. Not an easy chore, mind you, as I was still positive that strength, not agility, was a man's best friend.

Lesson No. 3: girls don't like to wrestle. Not in public, anyway.

After that loomed another problem. Not only was I younger than my peers — and most girls dislike going out with younger boys — I was also only about five feet high.

My sister sarcastically said if I waited for a circus to come to town I might get a date with a lonesome midget. But she finally relented and found me a date.

Lesson No. 4: always be nice to your older sister.

As time went by and I had learned the Big Apple and once stunned my cronies by winning a jitterbug contest (my date was a strong girl so she did most of the work), my big moment came.

I guess I was 14 pretending to be 17 when one day my sister presented me with a crisis. There was a formal dance that night and at the last minute a friend of hers had been stood up.

And she would do anything, simply anything, to get to that vital formal.

The "anything" she would do, it turned out, would be go to the dance with me.

Lesson No. 5: never take a girl literally.

Uncle Arthur's tux had seen better days, and better shoulders, but it would do. But half-way through the formal I got a mite fed up — it was a stuffy affair, really.

So I told my date that a bunch of my friends were playing some pretty good jazz in a converted barn a few miles out of town. And if her car . . .

45

She was very understanding. She said something like, "Migawd, anything to avoid my friends seeing me here . . ." So away we went.

When I got home my sister and mother were both anxiously waiting up for me. Where had I been? What had kept me so late?

When I explained, both sighed with relief and finally asked me if I had enjoyed myself. When I said sure my mother, my very own mother, asked:

"Did you kiss her goodnight?"

Lesson No. 6: a boy's mother has no right to talk like that.

So, as I said, schools have been supplying sex education of a sort for a long, long time.

Mar. 16, 1971.

A sad end to a varied career

AN EAST COAST CANADIAN PORT — (CP) — The former luxury liner Queen Elizabeth, carrying more than 17,000 Canadian soldiers and airmen, has arrived safely in Britain, it was announced today. She sailed from here about a week ago.

Not being of a mathematical turn of mind, I have no idea how many times my two typing fingers pecked out

those immortal words during the early days of World
War II.

But I do know that even if the phrasing became stereo-
typed, between a combination of censorship and repetition,
I always got a bit of a thrill when performing this chore.

The Queen E had made it again, and another contingent
of Canadians had escaped the U-boat blockade of the North
Atlantic.

Naturally, practically everybody in those days, including
the Germans, knew that An East Coast Canadian Port was
a bureaucratic euphemism for Halifax. Because that was
practically the home port for the massive Queen E during
the early 1940s.

That is where she rested for a few days while incredible
numbers of young men and women clambered aboard for
the Atlantic run.

It would be rather mushy, and even unseemly, for anybody — even somebody who was a very youthful and im-
pressionable waterfront reporter during those days — to say
he loved the Queen E.

She was too big, too fast, too much of everything, for
love. But even so, when the news came that she had met a
fiery end in Hong Kong, there must have been quite a few
Canadians who felt a sense of loss.

As I said, you couldn't love that ship. Nobody can love
a ship when he is one of some 17,000 bodies jammed into
her interior. There are too many people in too little space
—most of them apprehensive about the trip ahead.

But you never forgot her. I can still recall the thrill of
watching her manoeuvre into her Halifax berth.

Naturally, her arrival was supposed to be a secret. But
from practically any part of the south-western part of the
city anybody who wished could see that large superstructure
— towering far above the dock sheds — inching in until
it seemed to fill the sky.

47

Even before that, anyone with eyes, and even a cursory knowledge of the waterfront, would know she was due. What other single ship demanded so many supplies ready in a single spot?

Then, of course, there was the never-diminishing thrill of her departure. Usually she cast off just before dawn.

The bustle was incredible. Hawsers were splashing in the water as they were loosed. The tugs, almost invisible in the special blackness close to her vast hull, maintained a constant whistle refrain as the captains kept in touch with the Queen E bridge way up there above them.

The supreme moment came when, finally out in the stream, the Queen E wished to cast off and be on her own. At that moment her great siren let loose with two mournful blasts.

You didn't hear those blasts as much as you felt them. The whole waterfront shook — and people in Halifax a mile away would waken briefly to realize that once again the Queen E was making an Atlantic dash.

But I think my special memory of the Queen E came one early summer morning. I was in a flying boat with a navy photographer who wanted some shots of the great ship at sea. We caught up with her just as the sun came up.

She was at full speed. At her prow a wave some 30 to 40 feet high was creaming away. As we came in low for a broadside shot we could look right through this bow wave — and the sun, for several minutes, turned it into one vast, beautiful rainbow.

It is a nice memory to have about a ship which will never again be duplicated.

Jan. 11, 1972.

Of beans and booze

But it is Sunday," my mother protested as she watched the waitress place a cold, crystal-clear martini in front of me "And this is Murray's."

That was her reaction when she learned that Murray's Restaurants had finally allowed drinks to be served. And she was upset.

It was bad enough when the bone-dry area in which she had spent her whole life went wet and a decent woman didn't know where to eat without being exposed to the sight of people drinking booze.

My mother had survived this traumatic experience only because there was one place that never changed — Murray's. There she was safe. There, too, she could demand to be taken for dinner when her son came visiting because there her son would not be able to have his inevitable martini.

But then it happened. One day she decided to celebrate my most recent visit by going out for Sunday dinner. At 12 noon we were ushered to our table because with mother dinner is served at noon and supper at 6 p.m. — a body's stomach clock doesn't change just because eating fads do.

My mother was busy looking around to see if she could spot any of her friends, when the waitress softly asked if I would care for a drink.

"A real drink?" I queried in a near-whisper. "Like a martini?"

So the martini appeared and another of my mother's bastions of respectability crumbled.

However, like hundreds, perhaps thousands, of other Murray's fans she rolled with the punch because nothing else changed, really.

I mean, despite the discreet intrusion of liquor the same wholesome food, reasonable prices and courteous service prevails.

It is an institution in eastern Canada where practically everybody, except the very rich or the very poor, has eaten at one time or another. And where many, many people eat, day in and day out.

Like many eastern Canadians, eating during those first working years presented something of a problem for me. The appetite was there, but very often the money wasn't.

In search of food young working people could afford, we frequented an amazing collection of alleged eating spots.

For one entire winter, I recall, I lived almost exclusively on beans. That was not because I was such a devotee of the bean. It was because I had found a place where you sat in a chair, balanced your large bowl of baked beans and two slices of brown bread on a specially-built arm, and filled yourself to the brim.

All for 25 cents. Including coffee.

Believe it or not, that is a good memory. Others are not so good. At one eatery I was surprised on my first visit to watch a man douse his slab of apple pie with catsup.

I nudged my companion and asked if he had seen that. He shrugged and said: "Eat here for a while and you'll be doing the same thing."

I sometimes wonder what the ptomaine rate was among cub reporters in those days.

So Murray's, when I could manage such a treat on pay day, was a veritable paradise.

And it's nice to be able to report that it still is. I agree with my mother — some things should not change, or change very slowly and slightly.

In fact, there was only one Murray's I didn't like. That was the one an old editor of mine used as his execution chamber. Once you received an invitation to have lunch with him there, you automatically cleaned out your desk.

It was his idea of a genteel firing. Right after the ice cream and coffee — ZAP.

Then one day it happened to me. The fatal lunch invitation. That, through no fault of Murray's, was the most ghastly meal I ever tried to choke down.

Then the coffee came. The editor sighed with content, leaned back and said.

"I liked the way you handled that shipwreck assignment. How would you like . . ."

My nerves didn't stop twitching for a week. But, as I said, this was not the fault of Murray's.

Sept. 30, 1972.
Weekend Magazine

Be it never so humble

If you are the kind of person who has a butler's pantry, but no butler, and rooms equipped with buttons to push when the maid is needed, but there is no maid, then you will know what I am talking about.

You too, in other words, are a nut about old houses.

People acquire this nuttiness in a variety of ways. Some claim they now live in completely impractical old homes because they simply got tired of the antiseptic practicality of modern houses.

Others rattle around in great wooden arks or squeeze themselves into small stone homes because of their feeling for history.

But many of us live the way we do because we were brought up that way and firmly believe that all homes are old.

This expensive fact of life was forced upon me when my wife and I bought our home. We had spent weeks looking at the proper kind of home for a family of three.

It was all very depressing.

Then we were shown this three-storey, red brick home (12 rooms, counting the two bedrooms on the third floor) we did not need and could not afford.

Naturally, we bought it.

The only way I can explain this act of lunacy is to blame it on heredity. You see, I had a great-grandfather who, when he was in my position with one wife and one child to house, bought a large wooden home in Nova Scotia.

So I come by my lunacy honestly.

That house, incidentally, is still there. I spent my childhood throwing three-foot logs into its wood-burning furnace, sniffing the mouth-watering aromas coming from the oven of its monstrous, iron stove and working the kitchen pump which brought up water from the spring-fed well in its cellar.

As I said, the house is still there, although now there is an oil furnace, a modern stove and running water. And the last letter from my mother informs me that the old place looks just great.

With that kind of background it was only normal — if that word can be used — for me to look for something old and lived-in when it became my turn to pick a house.

Many people, I know, consider this love of old things a kind of madness. Happiness to them comes in a split-level package or a chromium and steel wrapping.

They are entitled to their opinion. But so are those of us who differ, the nuts of the nation who like to mix the business of living with a little honest nostalgia.

July 29, 1972.
Weekend Magazine

Loss of a dog . . . and memories

It is somewhat silly, I suppose, considering all the real trouble there is in the world, to spend even a little while mourning the death of a dog. But we have been together for about a decade now — and believe me, the house is going to seem kind of empty for a time.

Sure, this is sheer sentimentality. I should be worrying about the mortgage, the state of affairs in Viet Nam, the hungry of the world. Well, I do think about those major issues, but for a short while most of my brooding will be taken up by a small black and white cocker spaniel that once answered to the name of Happy.

Happy was a Yankee, a Connecticut Yankee to be precise. We bought him when I was working in New York and living the harsh life of a Connecticut commuter. And in that area — known as "the mink belt" — buying a dog is not the easiest thing in the world.

First, of course, the kennel owner had to look at my pedigree (a rather startling experience for the one doing the looking) before showing me a dog. Finally Happy was produced. "He was the runt of the litter," the man in charge told me, an assurance, I guess, that the two of us should have a lot in common.

We did, too. At least, after a few weeks we did because it took a little while for Happy to establish the proper dog-master relationship.

During this time we had our crisis moments. The first came when our veterinarian, accustomed to dealing with Connecticut dog owners, looked me straight in the eye and said Happy needed psychiatric care.

"A psychiatrist?" I asked. "For a pup? Just because he scratches a lot? I came to ask you to give him a real good medicinal bath. I think he's picked up something."

After that somewhat unnerving experience I tried to get the idea through his thick puppy skull that if he would only listen to me, his dog's life would be a good one. But occasionally he would rebel.

At these times, when I was attempting to train him to obey a few simple orders, he would tire of the routine and skip across the street to nestle up beside a man-eating wolf a neighbor of mine kept under the mistaken impression that he had a nice watchdog.

I would go over to retrieve Happy, saying stupid things such as "nice dog," and the nice dog would curl his lip, show teeth eight inches long, and beneath this frightening expanse of strained ivory Happy would sit and dare me to come and get him. So early in life Happy learned that his master was a bit of a coward.

He also had a thing, apparently, about taking out Canadian citizenship. On our return we had to stop at the border to straighten up all kinds of details and while I was talking to our kindly border custodians Happy jumped out of the car and headed over the snow-covered fields in the general direction of Connecticut.

However, once here he settled in nicely and as long as

his food dish was always full and I remembered not to speak harshly, he was everything a dog should be. It was kind of nice having him in the house — no matter how late it was when I came home at least one member of the family was ready to leap in the air out of pure joy and dole out a few welcome back kisses.

As wives seem to have a thing about doing this, especially at 3 a.m., it is pleasant to have a dog to assure you that you are wonderful.

As I said, the death of a dog is not really of any importance. And I know it. Except that I kind of figure every person who has ever been owned by a dog will understand and forgive me for carrying on this way.

Jan. 8, 1966.

Part 11

MY FAMILY

or

My mother-in-law moves in mysterious ways

Occasionally when a fellow gets to living it up in the big city his ego can get out of hand. But I don't have that problem. Whenever my ego starts swelling a bit all I have to do is recall the day I came in the back door and my mother-in-law bustled into the kitchen to see who it was. When she saw me she shouted to my wife and daughter, "It isn't anybody. It's just Frank."

My wife's a "pre-worrier"

The other morning I went into the kitchen after breakfast and found my wife working furiously at the table with sheets of paper filled with pencilled notations six inches deep around her. Naturally, I made the mistake of asking her what she was doing.

"It's terrible," she told me. "Just terrible. Our daughter will never pass her mathematics next year."

My wife, you see, is what I call a "pre-worrier." In other words, she anticipates by months and years what to worry about. She is not content with today's worries, or even tomorrow's worries. She is already doing next year's worrying.

On this occasion, when I tried to calm her by pointing out that our daughter had always done well at school, and as far as I knew would continue to do so, my wife refused to be placated. And eventually I learned why.

My daughter, a few days before, had picked up her next year's mathematics text book from a friend who no longer needed it. My wife opened it and discovered she could not solve the problems. So immediately she was convinced that this meant our daughter would not be able to do them either.

"Don't be silly," I said. "I wasn't able to work out her mathematics problems last year. And she did just fine."

But my wife was not having any of this kind of reasoning. She had something real solid to worry about and, by golly, she was going to do some first class worrying.

"If she fails mathematics at this point," my wife pointed

59

out, "it means she will probably never really master mathematics. And then she will have a hard time getting into college."

Then, noticing that I was poking around in the refrigerator looking for something to chew on, she added:

"But you don't care. Here is your only daughter unable to go to college and all you can ask is 'where did you hide the apples?' What kind of a father are you?"

It was no use explaining that the college crisis would not be with us for another five years, or that my daughter had excellent teachers who would probably see to it that she mastered elementary algebra. I know my wife when she is in a mood to worry, and at such times sweet reason is not for her.

Why, I remember an occasion just before we were married when she told me brightly, "Just think, my boss told me I could go back to work any time I wanted." And when I asked her why she was planning to return to work even before she had quit work she said:

"Well, I'll be quitting work a few years after we are married but then there will probably be periods when you are unemployed or too sick or too old to work and it is nice to know that I can always get a job."

My starry-eyed-bride-to-be had yet to say "I do," and already she was looking at me as a sick, old unemployable guy whose brave wife would have to earn the family bread.

I knew there was no sense in trying to divert her. The only thing was to get her so immersed in another worry that she would forget this one. So I said:

"It wasn't algebra that bugged me in school. It was trigonometry. Boy, that was a real problem."

"Trigonometry!" my wife gasped. "I had forgotten all about trigonometry. And in about three years our daughter will have to take trigonometry. What will she ever do?"

Frankly, I really don't know how my daughter will do

when faced with trig. But I do know that we hear no more in the house about the horrors of algebra. My wife is no longer worried about current school problems — her entire worry mechanism is focused well in the future.

Which gives me and my daughter about three years in which to relax.

June 27, 1964.

Some things are best forgotten

There once was a time when I chuckled at the comment:

"Parents worry about their children because they are afraid their children will do what they did at that age."

But then one becomes a parent — and the whole thing does not seem so funny.

The other night, for instance, I came home and found I could not crash into my favorite easy chair in the living room. The living room was occupied.

So it was into the kitchen. My wife, when I cried about discrimination, explained calmly that our daughter had friends in the living room and they certainly didn't want me sitting there in my stockings.

"But I like talking to young people," I replied. "I like to hear what they say."

My wife raised an eyebrow and queried: "How you can hear what they have to say when you do all the talking?"

I sulkily retreated into silence. Then my daughter swished out into the kitchen and mixed a couple of drinks.

"They're drinking in there," I informed my wife. "Those kids are boozing it up — with my booze."

My wife asked me if I remembered how old my daughter was. Then she said:

"What has happened to the vehement liberal? Remember when you shouted that if a kid was old enough to go into the army, he was old enough to vote — or drink?"

Yes, I remembered, but only vaguely.

So my wife explained that as my daughter and her friends were operating under the new, relaxed rules that my generation had brought about, they were behaving accordingly.

"Our daughter is old enough to vote, under the new rules, and under the new rules she is old enough to drink," she said.

I could see I was trapped. When I was vociferously campaigning for lowering the voting age, and the drinking age, it never occurred to me that some day this would mean that my daughter, and her friends, would be drinking *my* booze.

What I envisaged was a liberated age when the kids of 18 and over would be able to go into a bar and buy a drink — with *their* money.

Obviously I had not considered all the ramifications of my viewpoint.

Then, wafting down the hall, came the sound of laughter and indications that a good time was being had by all.

"What do you think they are doing?" I asked my wife.

She remained so unruffled it was downright nauseating. "They're having fun, enjoying themselves," she said.

"But what are they *doing?*" I enquired.

"Well," my wife speculated, "what did you and I do at that age?"

"Migawd, we've got to stop that," I screamed. "Go in and throw them out. My own daughter, carrying on like . . ."

"Like you did," my wife finished for me.

My wife suggested I go to bed.

"Go to bed?" I questioned. "With a full-fledged orgy going on in my living room? Listen to them — and *your* daughter is still coming back and forth getting drinks."

"The kids have had about two drinks in three hours," my wife said, with that calm that was driving me out of my ever-loving mind. "In the same time you've had about five."

"That's unfair," I defended myself. "I'm in a highly nervous state. And I must say I'm very disappointed in you — why aren't you doing something about this sort of thing. Throw them out, rescue our daughter."

At this point the kitchen door opened and the kids came in. One and all said goodnight very nicely.

After they had left my wife asked:

"Now you can go to bed and recall how you behaved at their age."

"No, no," I said. "Just let me go to bed and go to sleep."

Family trends in electioneering

When I read that Mrs. Trudeau had fainted recently while listening to one of her husband's speeches, I think I understood how she felt, and he felt.

My wife, for instance, has had to listen to few of my speeches and believe me, this is something no wife should have to endure.

Mind you, I am not attempting to suggest that any speech I make might rank in importance with a speech made by our prime minister.

But, as far as my wife is concerned, the terror quotient is the same.

This aspect of public speaking had not occurred to me on that ill-fated occasion when I agreed to make my first oration.

It obviously had not occurred to my wife either, because she thoughtfully coached me so I would be the Demosthenes of the church basement speakers' league.

The first part went all right. But then I found my wife's face in the audience and noticed that she was silently mouthing each word with me.

This sight so fascinated me I forgot my place and jumped a few paragraphs. So imagine my surprise when, just when I was telling my most solemn and touching anecdote, my wife broke out in loud laughter.

Later I learned that she wasn't listening to me. Instead, she was reviewing the speech mentally and hadn't noticed that I had dropped out the funny part — so she laughed on cue.

Loyalty such as that can ruin a marriage.

Anyway, after the vocal ordeal was over I asked my wife what she thought she was doing laughing in the wrong place. She wanted to know what I was doing changing the speech in mid-flight.

At that point we reached an accord. Never again would my wife listen to me make a speech.

But politicians wives can't or won't. In recent years politicking has become a family affair, it seems. At every meeting the politician's wife must be there, smiling bravely.

During the course of a six-week campaign, it seems to me, this smile must become a mite forced. And mid-September's bon mot could easily become mid-October's big bore.

But there is the start of another trend which is still young enough to be nipped in the bud. This is the tendency I note of meeting organizers roping in the children of the candidate.

This, I vow, should be stopped — not to ease the burden on the wife, but to keep the candidate from losing his sanity.

If there is one thing more painful than a wife being forced to listen to her husband's speech, it is the agony suffered by a father who is forced to make a speech in front of his children.

Days prior to the speech the children have told their father they know he will disgrace them all and make a fool of himself.

They have done this so effectively that when Daddy walks onto the stage he is agreeing with them. The palms of his hands are clammy, his shirt is sticking to his back and, worst of all, his mind is a complete blank.

He can't even remember which party he is working for.

All he can see are the faces of his children out there, waiting for the inevitable prat fall.

So, I say, keep the kids out of those campaign halls or campaign oratory will hit a new low.

Sept. 14, 1972.

Marital puzzle not solved

One of the many marital puzzles I have never succeeded in solving is the double standard as applied to the night out.

A wife, for instance, will announce: "Tomorrow night I am playing bridge," in a matter-of-fact voice, and is extremely put off if her husband mutters something to the effect that this makes her third night out this week.

But when a husband announces: "I won't be home until late tomorrow night," things are much different. His wife immediately looks as shocked as though he had announced he was joining the Foreign Legion and she would never see his pay cheque again.

"Tomorrow night?" she queries. "Surely you don't mean tomorrow night?"

When assured that he indeed does mean tomorrow night and what is all the fuss about, she has a variety of gambits. Tomorrow night, which has not been mentioned at all up until this moment, suddenly becomes the one night in the year, if not the up-coming decade, when the husband should not think of staying out late.

"I was thinking of having the Droolies over," the wife will say. "We owe them a drink."

Or she will make references to other husbands who never, never think of staying out late without giving at least a month's notice, preferably in writing.

The husband who makes the mistake of trying to prove his right to a night out through logic is hopelessly lost.

He will say: "But honey, you play bridge with the girls

at least one night a week — I merely want to play a little poker tomorrow night. The first time we've had a chance to get together in a month."

His wife will either ignore this or reply, completely irrelevantly: "We girls always drink tea when we get together."

No, logic is not the answer. Nor is an appeal to a wife's sense of (pardon the expression) fair play. To continue to harp on the theme that if she can go out to play bridge he should be able to go out to play poker will be about as effective as trying to knock down a stone wall with a toothpick. She will merely reply bitterly:

"Mary's husband says he likes her to play bridge. He doesn't begrudge her a little pleasure in life. But then Mother always told me you had a selfish streak. She spotted that the first time she met you. But no, I wouldn't listen. . . ."

I have always figured that maybe the way to solve this night out problem would be to use, at least once, the old shock treatment. To announce: "I won't be home until late tomorrow night, dear — you remember I told you about my beautiful new secretary? Well, she's finally consented to give me a date."

As I said, I have thought about this approach. But as I am a practicing coward, I must admit I have never used it. No sireee!

To do so would be to risk losing my wife — and my secretary.

So my partial solution to the problem is admittedly a chicken solution. If my wife announces she is going to play bridge tomorrow night I say: "How nice," and then try to figure out which of the boys will be free to join me on that night.

Oct. 30, 1965.

Love letters in the "quick-sand"

The dreary chore of closing up my wife's old home was complete. I walked through the almost empty rooms out of curosity and idly flicked open a drawer in an old dresser. And almost fainted.

There, stashed away in neat piles, were the letters, the cables, I had sent my wife from overseas during the war — florid protestations of undying devotion plus all those outlandish promises a fellow will make when he is young and in love and far away.

Hastily I attempted to scoop up the bundle of papers. I hoped that I could get them out and hidden under the garbage before anyone noticed me. But my luck was out.

My wife spotted what I was doing and naturally wanted to know what I had found. "Just some old stuff," I said. "Nothing of importance. I was just going to throw it out."

Perhaps my voice betrayed me. Because my wife demanded to have a look. "After all," she pointed out, "this was my grandmother's home. Not yours. Let me have a look."

She started sifting through the pile and soon began to laugh in a most unsentimental manner. "Listen to this," she said, and proceded to read in a horribly loud voice:

"Love you the mostest, strongest always."

"Well," I tried to explain, "I was only 22 at the time."

I was also, or so it seemed to me a couple of decades later, a particularly dough-headed 22. Why else would I be overcome with the urge to send a message of love everytime I got close to a cable office in those long-gone days?

My wife, while I brooded about these matters, continued to glance through the missives. "Here's the one that almost landed me in jail," she said, holding one up for my perusal.

This was a cable of such inanity that I, not my wife-to-be, should have been jailed for pure mopery. What had happened was that I had innocently sent it from England's south coast a couple of days prior to the invasion. Not unnaturally the cable company scanned this gibberish, figured it must be a code, and asked the cops to chat with the recipient at the other end.

The Mounties who took on this chore were finally convinced that my wife-to-be was innocent of any wrong-doing except for the crime of being engaged to a nit-wit.

Finally, my wife's snickers and caustic comments got on my nerves. "Most women," I said somewhat huffily, "keep these tender mementos tied with a pink ribbon and carry them always. You leave them in a drawer in your grandmother's home without a second thought."

My wife had an answer for that thrust, however. She explained that she must have left them when she rushed away to welcome me back home.

"After all," she said, turning those big brown orbs on me, "I was so excited at the thought of seeing you again I couldn't remember to pack everything, could I?"

This seemed very logical until she added:

"Also, I didn't want to carry these things with me. Anyone who saw them would probably call the cops again."

April 10, 1965.

69

Burglars beware

My wife, along with many other women, lives with the fixed belief that there is a vast network of burglars plotting to break into her home and make off with her treasures. Although why burglars would go to all this trouble I really do not know — the only time there is any money in the house is on the occasional day when my daughter gets her allowance and forgets to spend it that afternoon.

However, the burglar complex is a real thing with my wife and the result is that I cannot come in through the back door, even in broad daylight, without her asking if I have locked all the doors.

Frankly, if I were a professional burglar and proud of my skill, I would never attempt to enter my home via the back door. It would be easier, and safer, to attempt to find one's way through the Brazilian jungle at midnight.

First, to enter the house this way, the garage door must be opened. And unless the person who enters is aware of this door's peculiarity he is simply asking for trouble. The door slides up easily enough but when the unwary or the unknowing person lets it go — it slides back down again. And unless our burglar is wearing a tin helmet he is going to pick up a nasty bruise.

Once inside the door the burglar, unless he wishes to climb over the top of the car, will have to move to the left. If he moves to the right he will impale himself on some large nails which were driven into the side of the garage years ago for just this purpose. At least, that is the only purpose I can figure.

So he steps to the left. And unless he puts his arm up smartly the handle of the lawn mower will swing out from the wall to rap him sharply across the jaw. I know this will happen because even though I live there, and use this entry only in broad daylight, I have yet to find a way to crawl over the lawn mower without disturbing it.

After that we will assume that we have a very experienced burglar on our hands and he will navigate the narrow channel between the garage wall and the car without knocking down a rake or shovel or hoe. But then comes his big test.

To get into the passageway leading to the house he has to go through a door on his left. This lets him into a small, dark cubicle with two identical doors. If he opens the one on his right he will walk into a closet and probably wedge his foot into a pile of flower pots. If he makes the proper turn, a half turn to the left, he will have the proper door — but when he opens it he will find there is not enough room in the cubicle for both him and the open door.

He will have to back out into the garage, reach into the cubicle, open the proper door and then step quickly through it before it swings shut. And, as he will be moving quickly at this point, he will undoubtedly stumble on the first of four steps leading up into the cold pantry.

That is where the real fun begins. Because, as he stumbles on the first step, he will automatically reach up for something to hang onto. This means — and I know, believe me — he will automatically grab a rack which holds an old croquet set. The rack will tilt — it is not fastened to the wall very firmly — and out of it will shower croquet mallets and large wooden balls.

Tell me, have you ever been sprawled out, flat on your face, on a steep, narrow staircase while wooden mallets and balls rain down on your unprotected head?

Somehow I have a feeling my wife is worrying about the

wrong portal. Burglars may force their way in through the front door — and take a chance on being seen by our vigilant police — but they'll never make it through the back.

Aug. 4, 1964.

The rubber-tired wraith

Today we will consider the case of the tidy mother-in-law.

Sure, sure, a lot of people are saying that if this is the one thing I can complain about when it comes to a mother-in-law, I'm lucky. And I'll go along with that. My M.I.L. is really a doll — except that she insists on having everything in its place, whether she knows that place or not.

Most of her efforts to keep my home in tickety-bo shape (she's convinced that without her we would all be up to our hocks in refuse in no time) usually do no more than confuse me.

I'll decide I want a drink, for instance. So I go to the cupboard in the kitchen, take out a glass and then rest the glass on the side of the sink while I go to the refrigerator to get some ice cubes.

And when I come back with my ice cubes, lo and behold, there is no glass. It is back in its place in the cupboard.

Some people might say that I should tell my M.I.L. to leave the glass alone. But my M.I.L. moves with all the noise of a rubber-tired wraith and can spirit herself from her bedroom upstairs to the kitchen and back upstairs again before I even know she is in motion.

One thing that really bugs my M.I.L. is a running tap. I often turn on a tap for a glass of water and let it run in the hopes that it will get cold and perhaps purify itself in the process — a futile hope, I know.

But not with my M.I.L. around. The minute she hears the sound of running water she is coming in like a retriever after a wounded duck. The first drop has hardly hit the basin before she is ghosting onto the scene, hand outstretched to shut off the tap.

Also, in my house, it is sometimes almost impossible to get dressed. I will pull a suit out of the closet and place it on the bed. Then I go into the bathroom.

And when I come out, the suit is gone. I dig it out of the closet again. Then, just before I put it on, I race downstairs to get the clean shirt I forgot.

Back up the stairs I whisk — too late. The phantom has struck again. My suit is back in the closet and have you ever tried to get dressed while all the time hanging onto your shirt, keeping a wary eye on your shoes and standing on your socks?

As I said, this sort of thing merely confuses me and I only turn purple in the face because my family expects me to turn purple in the face every so often. Just to make sure my blood is circulating, or something.

But Sunday my tidy M.I.L. almost did me in. Honest.

I had brought home the Christmas tree for the sun porch. Twelve feet high and a mass of solid ice it was, so I decided the only way to get it from the car and into the porch would be for me to walk backwards dragging the monster by its butt.

To facilitate things I went to the porch and unlocked and opened the front door. Then back to the car to start to drag the heavy tree after me as I backed slowly up the walk.

I backed carefully up the steps. And was a little surprised to feel the just-opened door against my shoulder

73

blades. However, I knew I had unlocked it and figuring the wind had blown it to, I swung back against the door to push it open again.

But it didn't give. I did. As I pressed my back against the door the leverage got to my feet, which obviously were standing on a skim of ice.

After I picked the spruce twigs out of my mouth and got back onto my feet, I turned to that immovable door and beat on it, screaming:

"Who locked this blankety-blank door. If someone doesn't open this blankety-blank door I'm going to . . ."

At this point, just before my fists splintered a panel or so, my M.I.L. opened the door.

"Oh, it's you," she said. "It was a lucky thing I came out just a couple of seconds ago — some idiot had left this door open. Yes, if I wasn't here to look after things heaven knowns what would happen."

And she might have a point at that.

Dec. 13, 1966.

Phone home for trouble

For years it had always been my policy never to phone home to announce I would be late. Mind you, this caused my wife, and any other wife who knew about this habit, to castigate me as some kind of a matrimonial sadist.

You know that wifely plaint:

"The least you could have done was phone — there was the roast turning cold and no word from you. Why don't you phone?"

Well, I had a very good reason for not phoning. This

reason was that I don't think a man should take on two fights when one fight will do.

I will explain. The husband who listens to his wife and phones home to say he will be late for dinner is asking for double trouble.

He will have a fight when he phones his wife. And then, when he does get home, he will have another fight.

My "no phone" technique eliminated half the trouble. By not phoning, I made sure that I would have only one fight — when I eventually reached home.

But apparently there is something written into the marriage contract — a clause no male eye is able to detect — which obligates a husband to phone home if he is to be late for the evening joint. So my wife, and everyone else's wife, or so it seemed, eventually got to me and weakened me to the point where I recently decided to change my age-old practice.

So the other night, as I chatted with the boys in a small tea room I happen to frequent, someone mentioned it was nearly seven o'clock.

"My goodness," I exclaimed, "I must call my wife and tell her I will be a little late for dinner. You know how wives are, they appreciate these little courtesies."

So I phoned. When my wife answered I said:

"Hello dear, just thought I'd call to say . . ."

"You're in jail," my wife shrieked.

"No, no," I assured her "I merely phoned to say I would be a little late tonight."

"Why did you phone tonight?" my wife asked. "You've been late for 20 years."

"Look, honey," I replied, "for all those 20 years you have been telling me to phone. You always said, 'if only you'd phone I would feel better about you being late.' So I'm phoning. I'll be home late tonight."

There was a lengthy silence and then I heard my wife scream: "Ahhhhhhhh."

75

"What's the matter?" I asked. "Are you all right?"

"The gravy splashed over onto the burner," my wife said.

"I don't understand," I said.

"There's only one of me, you know," my wife replied. "When you phoned I was stirring the gravy so I had to bring the phone over to the stove so I could continue to stir the gravy — after all, you can't let gravy just sit there or it will burn — so while I was listening to you I kept stirring but I was so startled by your phone call I stirred a little too vigorously — and, oh for heaven's sake, now the potatoes have boiled over. . . ."

For the next few moments there was dead silence. But I hung on grimly. Eventually my wife came back onto the phone to say:

"I don't know how you expect me to talk to you and get dinner. What did you call about?"

"Never mind, dear," I said. "I'll tell you all about it later."

July 15, 1967.

Perhaps we should rename Labor day

T he one drawback to having a working wife, as far as I can see, is that a long weekend allows her guilt complex to flourish.

Suddenly she is certain that she has been neglecting her

76

home and family and spends the three-day holiday wrapped in a cloud of dust.

This, naturally, has changed my view of a long weekend considerably. There was a time when I looked forward to such occasions.

We could go on a small trip. Or I could spend three days loafing around the house. Either way it was a good feeling.

But no longer. When this Labor Day weekend approached, for instance, I tentatively asked what we might be doing.

"Well, first," my wife said, "we'll clean out the attic."

That was not quite the answer I had expected. Why should we clean out the attic?

As soon as I asked that question I knew I had made a mistake. That attic was apparently in terrible shape.

"I haven't been up there for months," my wife complained. "I hate to think what I will find."

But apparently there is some immutable law that says an attic has to be visited every so often and all bats and other such debris cleaned out.

"Then," my wife added, "I think you should do something about the basement."

Obviously my wife was losing her mind. That basement is roughly the size of a football field. It is also very gloomy and has all kinds of mysterious crannies and cupboards.

My policy is to never go near the place. I don't really believe in trolls. But I also believe in not taking any chances.

But my wife ignored my shocked expression. "After that," she went on, "you can help me take down the drapes."

"Whatever for?" I asked. "They look perfectly okay to me."

My wife gave me a look full of contempt. "They're dirty," she said. "But naturally you wouldn't notice."

Then she stood there pensively. "I suppose," I said, "you are now going to suggest that I put on the storm windows."

With that her eyes lit up, but finally she regretfully shook her head. "It is a little too early for that," she said. "But you can always put them up on the Thanksgiving weekend."

So the weekend began. It was organized like a military operation and was just about as peaceful.

The attic, as my wife had confidently expected, was such a disgrace that it kept her happily engaged for hours.

Far beneath her frenzied activities I puttered around in the one area of the basement where there is any decent light. Then, as there was nobody about, I pulled out an old deck chair and sat down and had a good read.

When I emerged I found the drapes had already been hauled from their moorings. "You should have called me," I told my wife piously.

"No, you were still busy in the basement," she said. "And I am so happy to have that place cleaned up I figured I could handle the drapes myself."

A neophyte husband might have felt a twinge of guilt at this point. But this old-time husband merely sighed with relief and opined that after all that hard work he needed something to quench his thirst.

When Monday night arrived my wife was weary, but her guilt feelings had been assuaged. She said: "It's good to know that everything is clean and tidy — I don't think a woman should neglect the house just because she has a job."

I agreed, and gave her added reassurance by saying that the Thanksgiving weekend would soon be here and she could paint the kitchen as a special treat.

Sept. 7, 1971.

Football ritual vs. wives

For a little while the other Saturday I believed my wife had finally picked up at least a bit of the mystique which surrounds the ritual known as "watching football on TV."

For quite some time now my wife, like several hundred thousand other wives in this fair land, has fought against the weekend football ritual. These wives have talked about the necessity of cleaning up the garden for winter, the imminence of death by freezing if the storm windows aren't put up, and dream up phoney errands of mercy — all in a fruitless effort to unglue the men folk from the Green Bay Packers, or the Jolly Green Giants.

So it came as a shock, a very pleasant shock, when my wife last Saturday greeted me when I came in at the magic hour — 2 p.m. — and headed for the TV set with the words:

"Phil called. He wants you to call back. But he warned me that you weren't to call when you might interrupt any touchdowns."

I paused in mid-stride. A wife — my wife — showing some solicitude about a husband's sacred football viewing habits? Could it be true?

You're sure he doesn't want me to call right away?" I asked.

"No, of course not," my wife replied. "You know the game is just starting and Phil doesn't want to be disturbed. Wait until after the game."

I was so dazed, so over-joyed, I fumbled the TV dial and almost missed the kickoff. It was unbelieveable, but my wife was actually getting the message. Football was not to be interrupted.

I snuggled down into my easy chair. A husband doesn't win many victories on the marital front. But when he does — well, it's heaven.

So Russ Jackson faded back to pass. The ball was going to be a long one. It sailed on and on and on and . . .

"Why does Phil want you to call?" my wife asked at that moment.

"He caught it," I yelled, eyeballs bulging and glued to the screen.

"Phil's caught what?" my wife asked, coming into the room and standing between me and the TV screen. "Is something the matter with him?"

"No, nothing that a punch on the nose won't cure," I muttered as I tried to peer through my wife and interpret what all that noise on TV meant. Had he gone all the way or had someone stopped him?

"What a terrible thing to say," my wife said. "Anyway, Phil is bigger and younger than you. You'd better be careful. Anyway, he sounded friendly enough when he called."

"Phil loves me," I almost sobbed, trying to manoeuvre my wife out of my field of vision. "We're soul buddies."

"Well," my wife said, now completely blocking the TV screen as she busied herself with fixing a bowl of flowers on top of the set, "I can't understand why you are so upset."

From behind her the TV noises told me yet another crucial moment was building up. So I decided to try logic.

"Look," I pleaded. "Why are you so considerate about Phil? 'Don't call him when you might interrupt any touchdowns' you told me. Why can Phil watch a football game in peace and quiet, and I can't?"

"My, you do carry on so," my wife said. "Here you are in your easy chair, watching football, and all you do is complain. I don't understand you."

With that she finished arranging the flowers and left the room. But in less than two minutes she was back with the vacuum cleaner.

"You just watch to your heart's content," she said. "But I have to do something about the dirt you've tracked in over this rug."

At this point I got up and headed for the phone.

"What are you doing?" my wife asked.

"I'm going to call Phil," I replied. "If I know anything about the wives' Mafia he isn't watching football either. Not even when the touchdowns happen. HIS wife is probably moving the living room furniture."

Nov. 4, 1967.

Whither thou goest she's going too

You know, there was a time when I really enjoyed a party. The kind of party where you got all duded up and joined the fellows in a rousing clambake.

But those parties, naturally, are a thing of the past. Now my idea of the perfect party is to sit with a cold drink in my hand, a good TV set in the room — the TV set showing the Boston Bruins at their nasty best.

The reason for this change is easy to explain. The men-only party is dead. Now all parties are mixed — it has something to do with equality, or so I am told.

So today when the word party sounds on the male

tom-tom, one knows that this means one has to take the wife. Now there is no excuse. The wife says, "Where you go, I go — yea, even to the flesh pots."

Naturally, as an obedient husband, I do not object to this.

But what I do object to is the turmoil these partying ventures now invariably create. I realize that for most people going to a party isn't all that traumatic an experience.

Yet somehow I feel that for me preparing for a party is only a slightly less complicated problem than planning a trip to the moon.

Last Friday is a good example. On Friday night there was a good party planned. For some years this particular low-key orgy had been a "men-only" endeavour.

Looking back on those halcyon times, it seems to me I had no problems. I announced I was going to the party, my wife knew she couldn't go so she took no further interest in the affair, and I turned up.

But now, in keeping with this trend towards equality, women are also allowed to attend. This means my wife can go.

Now, about four days prior to the bash, my wife wants to know the state of my wardrobe. As I am a one-dinner-jacket, one-dress-shirt type of guy, I always assure her there is nothing to worry about.

And there never used to be anything to worry about.

But no longer. This year, the morning of the bash, my wife looked at my dress shirt and had an attack. When she recovered she asked if I really planned to wear that particular shirt.

"Naturally," I said. "I have been wearing that shirt for the past 10 years."

Obviously that was not the correct answer. Because the shirt was hurled into the trash.

Then my wife, doing an inventory, looked at my cummerbund. "Do you wear this?" she queried.

Well, I'm pretty proud of that cummerbund. It is the tightest cummerbund in town. At least, it is when I finally succeed in fastening it.

Then there was the matter of my black tie. I cannot tie a bow tie. Once a salesman tried to demonstrate how a bow tie was tied by knotting it about his leg.

I followed all the intricate moves easily, but for some reason my wife will not allow me to wear my bow tie a coy three inches above the knee.

So I had acquired one of those snap-on ties. As my wife tossed it on top of my discarded shirt she sneered:

"I guess you can take the boy out of Bible Hill, but you can't take Bible Hill out of the boy."

Anyway, the party suddenly became a major overhauling program. I left for work Friday morning with instructions to buy a new and decent dress shirt, a new and proper tie and a new and up-dated mental approach to parties.

Then at 3 p.m. Friday, the phone rang. It was my wife. Yes, I told her, I have a new shirt. Yes, I have a new tie.

Then she screamed, "Shoes — I bet you forgot shoes."

Wotthehell, I told her, I am already wearing shoes. But I should have known better. New shoes had to be acquired.

As I said, it was a swell party. I only wish I hadn't been so tired when I got there.

Jan. 26, 1972.

The true menace of Christmas

Perhaps today it would be appropriate to consider the Christmas tree as the greatest single agent for discord in any marriage.

You don't believe me? Well, stop trying to lick the pine pitch off your hand and think back to Christmas trees you have known.

Consider those early years of marriage. When your bride thought it would be great fun for the two of you to go and pick a tree. Togetherness is a big thing in those early married years — remember?

Anyway, the two of you went from tree lot to tree lot. Your bride simply couldn't find a tree that was HER tree. "Our tree," I believe the term was.

So it was 30 below with a sharp wind. And at the 11th tree lot you said: "Whattayamean it is too skinny? Let's buy the damn thing and go home. I'm frozen."

Yes, that's generally the way the first Christmas tree fight gets started.

But there are many other ways. As the years go by, and togetherness is not all that big a thing, your wife will go through the phase of believing that unless YOU rush out and buy a tree the very first weekend the tree lots appear — well, you'll end up with a decorated broom as your tree.

So it is Sunday afternoon. There is a merry old time on the Packer's five-yard line. And your wife looks in and screams:

"Whattayamean sitting there? Get out and buy that tree. They'll all be gone. Hurry, hurry."

It could be that is how that second Christmas tree fight gets started.

One might believe that going out and getting a tree on one's own would eliminate much of the Christmas-tree generated discord. But that is not so.

True, the husband does not have to trek from lot to lot, slowly turning blue. He can drive up to the first lot he finds, lean out the window of the well-heated car and say:

"Hey Mac, gimme one about seven feet high and stuff it in the trunk, huh."

He doesn't even have to get his ears chilled.

But coming home is another proposition. All young wives, apparently, were brought up in homes where the fathers always had trees so symmetrical and round and full and bushy it is a wonder the girls could bear the thought of leaving home. Because no young husband has ever brought home a tree without his wife saying:

"But it's so little, and skinny. And well, I don't know how you could have picked up a tree like that."

Which is pretty well guaranteed to touch off Christmas-tree-fight number three.

As the years go by and the wives mellow (of course they mellow, otherwise all husbands would run away from home), the Christmas tree gambit becomes a little more subtle.

Then, when a husband comes chugging home with the tree of his choice, the wife doesn't make any really snide comments.

She merely walks around the tree, says, "You mean you paid $6.50 for that?" and breaks into gales of hysterical laughter.

Which could very well start Christmas-tree-fight number four.

85

The real crisis about the Christmas tree occurs, however, at the stage when the average husband thinks things have levelled off somewhat. This is when the couple has moved out of an apartment and moved into something known in the women's magazine as "a home of your very own."

At this point your wife not only wants a symmetrical, round, full and bushy tree for the living room. She wants, as she puts it, "a tree out on the front lawn — about 20 feet high and covered with lights."

Your comment, as a husband, when you hear this is "you must be smack out of your cotton-pickin' mind." So the very next weekend, a sleety, gusty Sunday, who is out on the front lawn, wrestling with a 20-foot high tree and 25 strings of lights?

You know who is out there. And you also know that the fight started by this kind of a Christmas tree can make any other Christmas-tree generated-fight look like a prelim bout in the Golden Glove bantam class.

But what the heck. It's Christmas, isn't it? And if it was all sweetness and light the whole thing would get a little cloying.

Dec. 19, 1967

On facing up to a storm crisis

One of the main troubles with being an adult male is that when a crisis hits, people expect you to do something.

They never know what one should do. They merely look at you and finally one of them — usually your wife — shouts, "Don't just stand there. Do something."

My problem is that when a crisis occurs I would like to do something, but I am never sure just what this something should be.

I could let out a full-bodied scream of terror, I suppose. But that doesn't seem to be what is expected of me.

This thought comes to mind because the other night a crisis came about. I had just reached home, about 7:30 p.m., and was sitting in my easy chair with my "welcome home" martini in my hand.

Then, just as I lifted the martini to my lips, there was a blinding flash, an explosion — and the house was plunged into darkness.

I might add here, to show how cool I can be, that I lifted about three feet out of the armchair. But I did not spill a drop of my martini.

As I sat there in the darkness, sipping thoughtfully, there were a few moments of blessed silence. Then, sure enough, my wife said:

"Don't just sit there. Do something."

I mulled over that order. Just what was I supposed to do? For instance, if all that commotion had been caused by a bomb set off by an irate reader outside my house, was I supposed to go out and check into the matter.

Not bloody likely, I thought to myself.

So I sat and sipped.

But my wife wasn't happy with this arrangement. "Find some candles," she ordered.

Now why would I know where the candles were hidden? Candles in our home are usually used only on the dining room table and, as the dining room table is my wife's domain, it seemed to me that she should know where the candles were.

87

A sensible deduction, no?

No.

As I rummaged around looking for candles, I happened to glance out the kitchen window. Then I knew what had happened.

Out there, on top of the snow, power lines were writhing and spitting out sparks.

"Don't worry," I told my wife cheerily. "All that has happened is that the ice has slid off the roof and snapped our power lines."

My wife replied:

"Well, do something."

That was a poser. What did she have in mind? Was I supposed to go out there in the dark, burrow around in the snow, and with my bare hands splice those power lines back together?

Me? And I can't even change a fuse.

Anyway, as I was standing there pondering whether I should face up to my wife's wrath, or face up to being electrocuted, a kindly policeman came along.

He sized up the situation immediately, called an emergency Hydro crew, and two hours later we were back in business.

"See," my wife said later, "there are some men who can do something."

As I said, this is what happens in a crisis. Other people are allowed the luxury of panic — but not me.

Once, I recall, my wife and I were on a train. The train got stuck in an over-size snow drift. This was carefully explained to the passengers by the crew — so I put my feet up and prepared to wait it out.

But not my wife. She turned on me and indignantly queried:

"Well, aren't you going to do something?"

The sheer idiocy of this question left me speechless. Do something? Go out and push?

So I closed my eyes and did what I do best in any crisis. I tried to go to sleep.

Mar. 6, 1971.

Crisis in the church

Church suppers.

That was when all the good things from the harvest were put together by the ladies of the church and for a modest fee people for miles around could come and eat some of the finest food imaginable.

At least, that is what our memories told us.

But I have a more recent perspective on church suppers. A few years ago my wife was recruited to work at one.

The first shock I received came when she told me the menu — a meal built around spaghetti and meatballs. This, compared to my memories which insisted that only roast chicken or baked beans — supported by all the fresh vegetables which had just been taken from the gardens of the neighborhood — could be served in a church.

But after this particular supper was over, and my wife sat with her eyes closed, I got the inside story about present-day church suppers. And it was quite an exposé.

We'll ignore the introductory disasters, and move right into the part where the spaghetti meat sauce, with the meatballs for 150 dinners, burned. The sauce could not be salvaged — a rush order to a nearby restaurant solved that problem — but the thrifty ladies decided that the meatballs *must* be saved.

So they took each meatball (300 in all) and held it under a tap until the burned portion disappeared.

All this excitement so unnerved one of the volunteer supper workers that she got really confused. After the well-washed meatballs had been served in their store-made sauce ("Nobody complained," my wife said) this willing slavey remembered she had forgotten to put the whipped cream on the slices of apple pie.

She dashed to the refrigerator, grabbed a bowl sitting there, and feverishly began daubing the slices of pie. More than 50 pieces of pie had been served before somone discovered that in her rush she had grabbed a bowl of mayonnaise instead of the whipped cream.

"It was pretty funny," my wife said in a voice which did not contain the least sign of hilarity, "to see 50 people, forks all poised, suddenly have their pie whipped out from under their noses."

Other than that, apparently, the supper was a success. As my wife said: "If it hadn't been for burning the sauce, we would have netted $15. But we're proud of the fact that tonight the church is only $5 poorer."

Oct. 11, 1969.
Weekend Magazine.

It's the wife who pays

F rankly, I have no way of knowing how this vignette will or will not fit into the continuing discussion about Women's Lib. So let us say that I am offering it only as a vignette — with no sociological implications.

It all started very simply. My wife, who has been a working gal ever since our single chick fluttered away from the nest, called and said she would like to have lunch with me.

Flattered — even after 27 years of marriage I can be conned into thinking my wife likes me as a luncheon companion — I agreed.

I must say she looked great when she came in. And perhaps I should explain here that when I have lunch with my wife, I always arrive about 20 minutes ahead of the appointed time.

The reason? Well, she is a one-martini lunch person and I am a two-martini lunch person. My 20-minute head start allows me to come out even.

So we had a delightful lunch. As a dedicated career woman she told me our daughter needed a cash infusion and would I please look after this detail?

She also handed over sundry bills which had to be paid and finally zeroed in on the fact that what we really needed in life was a new car.

As I always say, it is a delight to lunch with a career woman who is independent.

Finally, as has to happen with any lunch, the bill arrived. It dawned on me that I had not gone to the bank that day.

After glancing at the contents of my pocket, I made a mild request. "Have you got five bucks?" I asked. "I seem to be a little short. And I'll pay you back when I get home tonight."

Suddenly the warmth which had permeated this small family lunch dissipated. My wife wanted to know why I needed five dollars. Had I been fired?

I assured her that of that moment I was still employed. It was only a temporary case of the shorts.

She said she never carried any money. Meanwhile, she was nervously pawing around in her purse and letting bills scatter around.

I grabbed one and said, "Thanks for the fiver." Only to have it snatched out of my hand.

"I've never been so insulted," she said. "Usually when men invite me to lunch they pay the bill. But as you can't pay the bill, I will."

With that she triumphantly hauled out a credit card and presented it to the anxious waiter.

"See," she crowed, "I have credit cards, too. I will pay for the lunch — I don't need to borrow money."

"Don't forget to write in the tip," I said nastily.

"I always leave at least 50 cents," my wife replied, very righteously. "Two people — a quarter each."

While I mentally wrote off that place as a luncheon spa in the future, my wife left to go back to work. I did the same, and a few hours later was at home.

Much to my surprise my wife was furious.

"It just occurred to me," she said between clenched teeth, "that you also have a credit card. Why didn't you pay for the lunch with your credit card?"

I tried to explain but my career-minded, liberated wife shut me up saying:

"Don't you know that wives never, never pay for lunches?"

Feb. 12, 1972.

My FLOWERS

or

They never promised me a rose garden

One year not too long ago the Town of Montreal West — the place I now call home — gave me a pretty certificate for having "one of the 100 best gardens in the community." I felt pretty good about this until my wife mentioned there were only 99 gardens in the area.

Love me, love my yard

In this frenetic age everybody has to be on the move. I mean, you come into the office on a Monday and everybody wants to know how your weekend was.

And I have noticed that when I tell them I had a nice, quiet weekend at home, watching clouds drift by and maybe watering my roses, a certain chill sets in.

You know — you are an outsider. The fellow over there, the one on crutches, wants to tell you what a dandy time he had water skiing until that rock got in the way.

The girl who types standing up is eager to regale you with the joys of sunbathing.

They have all been doing something. While you, you creep, have been lolling around the house enjoying yourself.

However, I am in favor of the lolling-type weekend. To explain why, let's have a look at what happened to me, right in my own yard, last weekend.

At one point, while I was watering the lawn, a neighbor's seven-year-old daughter came to help. She watched the operation for a time, and then decided she could handle the hose more efficiently.

So she started. Almost immediately she found her progress was impeded by a snarl in the hose.

She wanted to know how this had come about. I told her it had just happened. So she gave the hose an impatient tug and looked up triumphantly to report:

"I just made it unhappen."

She also indicated that she has the instincts of a true gardener. She inspected my rose garden and sharply admonished several bushes she felt were not trying hard enough.

She knows instinctively that a rose needs an occasional "shape up or ship out" lecture to set it on course.

Two other visitors were a couple of kids who introduced themselves as Peter and Terry. Peter is the bigger of the two but Terry is stronger.

When they were kind enough to introduce themselves I told them my name. There was a pause and one of them asked: "Is your first name Frank?"

I assured him that was the case and he replied. "That's funny — most grownups don't have first names."

Another visitor, late Sunday evening as I was sitting in a deck chair looking at the dark, was a cat. Most cats don't like me. When I approach they haughtily walk away.

This one strolled across the lawn in the moonlight, gave me a searching examination, and jumped into my lap. Things like that kind of make a fellow feel he isn't all bad.

But the greatest thrill of my weekend was the aerial show. I don't know if you realize this went on, but last Saturday night there was one of those rare displays of Northern Lights.

As I sat there the lights began to bloom. At first they came and went so rapidly it was difficult to tell whether they were real Northern Lights, or perhaps reflections.

But finally they came on strong. A great canopy of light, like a gothic ceiling, spread over the night sky. It was a ceiling that moved and pulsated and constantly changed.

As I said, who needs to go away on a weekend when all this is happening?

June 23, 1972.

The watch on the rose

Every so often my sympathies are all with the hippies — those gentle if somewhat bedraggled souls who advocate that one should drop out of the 20th Century rat race. In fact, right now is one of those times, mainly because I feel the pressures are getting too great.

Not the pressures of my job, mind you.

What I am talking about is the pressures of my garden.

For some years now I have had a garden — mainly roses. It was kind of fun. If there weren't too many bugs and if I remembered to turn on the hose and if the kids didn't run through the bushes too often, I occasionally had a rose to cut and show to my wife.

She was very nice about it, too. She would invariably look at this rose with wide-eyed admiration and say something like: "You mean you really grew this — that after only 100 man hours of labor and $300 of fertilizer you grew this rose?"

I tell you, it is moments such as these that make gardening worthwhile.

But now I feel all the innocent fun has gone out of gardening. It started this spring when a bunch of self-appointed vigilantes in my small community decided to prod the peasantry into beautifying the joint in honor of Centennial year. Notices were sent out urging all of us to pep up our gardens and spend a couple of thousand bucks on painting the old hacienda to keep in step with the 100th birthday theme.

Naturally, I paid no attention to this.

The only attention my garden had ever received was to qualify — every year or so — as a possible recipient of dust bowl benefits. So I merrily continued on my amateurish way — planting bushes and then hoping that nature would do something about the whole thing.

Then the blow fell. The other night I went home and there waiting for me was a formal letter from our vigilantes in charge of beautification.

My wife handed it to me, saying:

"They have probably told you your garden is a potential health hazard and suggested you put in colorful, attractive flagstones."

But this wasn't it at all. The letter, when I succeeded in getting my eyes in focus, said:

"We are happy to inform you that your garden has been selected as one of the best 100 gardens in our community . . ."

"Quick," I asked my wife. "How many gardens are in our community?"

"Oh," she said, counting on her fingers, "about 99."

However, despite this niggling approach, that letter had a very upsetting effect. Prior to its coming it never occurred to me that my garden — and its success or failure — was of any concern to anyone but me.

Now when I venture out, rose dust in hand, I find myself peering surreptitiously around the neighborhood. Is a beautification vigilante watching me? Am I using the proper kind of rose dust? It is terribly unnerving.

Then, of course, my weekends are almost unbearable. There was a time, before I had to maintain a reputation as being one of the community's 100 best gardeners, when I would dash away with the family on a Saturday. And who cared about the weeds and the bugs and blooms?

Not now, though.

Now, when my family pleads, "please, it's a hot day and

we want to go to the lake and we haven't been away for a single weekend since that blasted letter arrived," I am adamant.

"It's all right for people like you who have never been competitive," I tell my family, "to talk about shirking your responsibilities. But what about me?

"What would people think if next summer I was not judged as having one of the best 100 gardens in the community? They'd say I was a has-been, that I was slipping. They might even say I was getting too old to continue to compete in the rose rat race. That's what they would say."

So ignoring the pleas, and even threats, from my family, I head out to the rose garden.

But sometimes, as I spray and dig and clip and crouch, I wonder if it is all really worthwhile. Does a man really have to be known as having one of the 100 best gardens in his community?

Is that all there is to life?

Or could he drop out? Could he become the hippie of the garden set and preach, "Make Love — But Don't Fertilize?"

July 22, 1967.

I can hear them giggling now

It makes me feel a little better to read that the United States embassy in London is losing its battle with bulb-eating squirrels.

99

Don't get me wrong. I am not one of those people who enjoys seeing the U.S. taking it on the nose.

It cheers me up only because if an embassy, with all that money and all that staff at its disposal, can't lick a bunch of squirrels, I should not feel badly because of what happened to me over the years.

After all, I have no money and have also had to conduct this battle without any help.

Perhaps you didn't see the news item to which I refer. It said the U.S. embassy this fall put in hundreds of crocus bulbs.

But as every gardener should know, crocus bulbs to squirrels are what caviar is to the Jet Set. In no time all those bulbs had been eaten up by squirrels, despite the best efforts of a legion of gardeners.

However, I realize how this all came about. About nine years ago when I first got entangled in a death grip with a mortgage, the one mitigating factor was that surrounding my house was a little bit of earth.

This brought out the homesteading instinct said to be a part of every Canadian. I looked at that beautiful bit of earth — "it's mine, all mine" — and decided that I would turn it into a bower of beauty.

Little did I realize that all I was really doing was setting up a free lunch for a bunch of furry, long-tailed rodents.

But that first fall in my new home I did not know that. With all the faith which only the completely ignorant can possess, I bought about 500 bulbs.

I also dug 500 individual holes — or should I say "bored" 500 individual holes, because nobody had told me that this alleged earth of mine was 99 per cent clay.

Into each hole I put some good earth, mixed this with a pinch of bone meal and some fertilizer, carefully placed a bulb and then tenderly covered it.

It only took me a week, and after three weeks I could

walk again. And all that winter I was picturing the glories that would be mine come spring.

Well, the spring finally came, as it does even in Canada. And I had my glories — 49 of them, to be exact.

But I wasn't going to let this deter me. The next fall I bought another 500 bulbs. I dug another 500 individual holes.

Only this time I not only put bone meal, fertilizer and a bulb in each hole. I also, after adding an inch or two of earth, put in some moth ball flakes before finally filling the hole.

Moth ball flakes, I was told, would drive away the squirrels. Once the critters dug down a few inches and got a whiff of those flakes they would vamoose.

That, at least, was what I was told. However, somebody forgot to tell my squirrels that they were allergic to moth ball flakes.

Because the next spring I had only about 70 bulbs produce.

But it was progress. So I persevered.

By last spring, by conservative count, something close to 4,000 bulbs had been buried around my house. And the yield was so skimpy my wife took one look at the results and said:

"This fall you really should plant some bulbs."

I didn't hit her. I merely said "yes dear," and this fall called in some professionals.

One man casually dug a series of big holes. Another followed him, tossing a handful of bulbs into each hole. A third followed and covered up the holes.

I watched aghast. No bone meal, no fertilizer, no moth ball flakes. No tender loving care.

And in the evenings I swear I can sit in my house and hear those squirrels chomping and chuckling because I am convinced that once again I will have lost.

101

But, as I said, now that I know that even the full might of the U.S. embassy can't lick a bunch of squirrels, I can listen to those festivities with a less heavy heart.

Dec. 3, 1970.

Be ruthless with your roses

At this time of year when people comment on my bent-kneed, sway-backed, Groucho Marx manner of walking, I reply with the single word: "Roses."

Non-rose lovers are bewildered by this. But rose lovers nod with understanding and sympathy.

They know that this is the time of year when a rose grower has to determine which of his roses have survived the winter, and which have (sob) been carried away to that great rose garden in the sky.

Unfortunately, there is only one way to perform this painful and ofttimes emotional task. That is, you have to get down on your hands and knees, place your nose as close to the bush as possible and try to discern a trace of green in the winter-blackened branches.

You try doing that for an hour or so, with your knees sinking into the cold, wet mud, and you too will be able to walk like Groucho Marx.

The painful part of this annual spring rite, however, is not the stooping nor the cold, wet mud. It is making that all-important decision as to whether or not a particular plant is dead or alive.

If the bottom part of the plant is all black, but there is a smidgin of green half-way up one twig, is the plant alive

102

and well? Or — oh, the agony of it all — does this mean it must be dug out and cast aside?

It is not an easy decision to make, let me tell you.

My wife, who likes roses in the house but has little feeling about them when they are outside, claims I carry on too much about this dead-or-alive bit.

She says that last Sunday she heard me two blocks away when I screamed, "It's dead, my beautiful white bush, dead, dead, dead."

Well, I see nothing to apologize for. After all, that particular bush represents about four years of my life. It wasn't a strong bush to begin with, but with tender, loving care it bloomed beautifully for three summers.

But no more, alas. As soon as I am able to steel myself, it will have to be dug out. But maybe, just maybe, if I delay a week a bit of green might show.

Wouldn't that be wonderful?

Naturally, I know that I am really postponing the inevitable. There are few miracles wrought in a rose garden, as any rose-fancier will tell you.

A rose garden, in fact, is a place of grim reality where most times the bad news outweighs the good news. It is no place for the weak and the indecisive.

I mean, just the other day I took a look at the third bush in the second row. Now this bush for many a year had provided me with big, deep red blooms.

And it is not true, as my wife claims, that after I dug up that particular bush I shut myself in my room to have a good cry.

After all that exertion I was tired. That is all. So I went to my room to rest.

Tears have no place in the rose gardener's arsenal, I always tell my wife. I keep blowing my nose only because I have a slight cold, which also makes my eyes water occasionally. So there.

What keeps us rose lovers going through this dismal

period is the knowledge that once the eliminating has been done, we can get on with the business of planting new bushes.

And have a few weeks of euphoria dreaming about the wonders to come.

May 11, 1972.

Skeptics beware — the roses may hear

In the summer of 1970 I wrote a column explaining why my roses were not doing as well as they usually did. My theory, as expounded at the time was that as I had been suffering a bad back, I could not give the roses the personal attention they needed.

Without me to personally encourage them, and sometimes threaten the more reluctant producers — "if you don't do better by next week I'll pull you out, roots and all" — the roses simply were not up to scratch.

Mind you, quite a few people scoffed. The true rose lovers didn't, of course. In fact, that column was reprinted in the Canadian Rose Annual. But non-rose people hinted quite strongly that I had finally, and predictably, flipped my wig.

But now I believe I have those scoffers where I want them. If these "realists" who claim there is no proof that flowers respond to flattery and threats will read on, they will find that there *is* proof .

First, do you know what a polygraph is? A polygraph is

a lie detector. It is an electrical gadget which is wired to a suspect and when the suspect answers questions the emotional reaction — heart beat, blood pressure — is recorded.

A little while ago a man who operates a polygraph was being interviewed on a TV show. He said that one day when he was about to water a plant he has in his office he got curious as to how quickly this water would get from the roots to the leaves.

As a polygraph when it measures the emotional response to a questions also indicates a sudden outbreak of sweat on the skin, the expert hitched his machine to the plant.

But he got more than he expected. The machine began to record almost human responses. When he watered the plant and talked in a normal tone, the recorded graph was normal, too.

But when he shouted, the graph jumped, just as it would if the polygraph was recording the reaction of a frightened human.

Then, when he lit a match and moved menacingly toward the plant, saying, "I think I will burn this plant," the graph almost blew itself off the paper. The machine indicated that the plant was terrified — or, to put it another way, the graph looked the same as that made by a terrified human.

Now, I realize this plant in question was not a rose. But I am assuming that as roses are far superior to any other kind of plant, they would also be more sensitive, more aware.

In other words, if an ordinary potted plant reacts in this manner, think of the turmoil there is in an ordinary rose patch.

If only we could tune in, it would be like walking through a boiler factory going at full speed.

But mainly this little story, or so I hope, will clear me of the accusation that when it comes to roses I am some kind of a nut.

Because, up until I heard about the polygraph experiment, I had been putting off writing about the performance of my roses this summer.

I had planned to tell how this summer conditions have been much improved. Because my back is much better, I have been able to be with my roses ever since spring.

I go out and talk to them regularly and administer little pats to the ones doing well, and give stern lectures to the laggards.

There is a yellow rose, for instance, that shakes in his humus each time I approach because, well, he hasn't been doing his thing properly. And I've told him so.

But I was a mite leery of telling you this, up to now, because I couldn't face up to the reaction I was sure would be forthcoming.

But now I don't worry. If anybody complains we will merely hire the nearest polygraph — and talk to the roses.

Aug. 17, 1971.

Part IV

CURRENT EVENTS

or

The media are the message

I was 13 years old when I first had a byline in a newspaper, The Truro Daily News. I wrote a column of Boy Scout news once a week. For a giddy six months I was the Walter Lippman-cum-Pierre Berton of the knee-pants set. Then I authored a scurrilous attack on our District Commissioner . . .

The old Canadian male

Recently the newspapers carried a lengthy account of a speech outlining the role of "The New Canadian Woman", and I had no objection to this at all until the speaker began to stray from her subject and talk about "The New Canadian Male".

She said, in this context, "the role of the father in the home has also changed. He no longer expects his pipe and slippers to be brought to him when he comes home from work, but in many cases pitches in and helps get the evening meal under way."

This kind of talk, I would like to say, is downright dangerous, if not subversive. I really don't think many husbands today dash home just so they can start preparing the evening meal.

What happens is that women speakers keep harping on this point hoping that men will start to believe that this is the way things really should be. It is the technique of the Big Lie — tell it often enough and people will believe it — and start doing it.

When I get home at night (if I get home) I don't bellow for my pipe and slippers, true, mainly because I don't smoke a pipe, and with the floor draughts the way they are in our old pile of bricks I keep my overshoes on most of the time.

But neither do I "pitch in" and help prepare the evening meal. My part in this ritual is confined to entering the kitchen, asking, "What's for dinner tonight?" and then making a sharp left hand turn which brings me smack in front of the refrigerator.

Then I figure that as I am in front of the refrigerator it would be a shame not to open the door and see if there are any ice cubes. And once I have learned that there are ice cubes I figure "waste not want not" and so use a few.

At that point I take my ice cubes, by this time nestling in a glass, over to the kitchen table and I sit there and watch my wife prepare the meal.

It is a most fair division of labor, I believe.

Also, in this way a husband and wife can have one of those little chats which do so much to keep marriage intact. I tell my wife about all the exciting things that happened to me during the day and she replies:

"Ouch, that pan is hot."

In this way we establish a rapport, an ideal which only a successful marriage can achieve. In other words, she doesn't listen to me and I don't listen to her. This cuts down on arguments.

Then, when the meal is served, I can hoe into it and add to the felicity of our union by being genuinely surprised. I can pay my wife one of those spontaneous compliments women love so much, such as: "Darling, it continues to amaze me the way you make a pound of hamburger last."

If I had "pitched in" and helped prepare the dinner, as the New Canadian Male is supposed to, I would not have been surprised. In fact, the fight would have started a half-hour sooner.

So I believe, despite this propaganda put out by females who desire to remodel the male and particularly the married male, that the old ways are best. They make for a much more peaceful home, honest they do.

Feb. 7, 1963.

Speed kills

Recently there have been reports in the newspapers about a new reading method that is being tried out, a method which will allow an ordinary reader to gulp down a book the size of Anthony Adverse in two hours.

And I say, who wants to?

One of the few pleasures left in this world is leisurely reading. It is a delightful sensation to realize, half way through a hectic afternoon, that there is a brand new book waiting at home — and a nice, long evening in which to read it.

Admittedly, I'm a little nuts when it comes to reading. If there is nothing left in the house to read I'll peruse the telephone book. At least it has more plot than most TV fare. This summer, when my store of books at the summer cottage ran out, I unashamedly purloined my daughter's collection of comics and Mad Magazines.

Even a cook book will do to wile away a lonely hour, but this usually leads to messy experiments in the kitchen and is to be recommended only as a last resort.

I haven't checked on the literary fare of small fry recently, but when I was a member of the slingshot and bubble gum set, Christmas would not have been complete without my copies of the Boys' Own Annual and Chatterbox. The one trouble with these mammoth tomes, packed with deeds of derring do, was that they were too large to be read conveniently by flashlight under the bed covers at night.

As an adult, I get an equal thrill — perhaps because it is also an illicit manner of indulging my passion — in using an afternoon when I should be working to browse through the book stores.

But apparently in this age we are too busy to read for enjoyment. We must learn to take our literature in quick gulps, just like medicine.

The account of this new reading method stated that those who practiced it were able to remember what they had read. But pure memory is no guarantee of reading enjoyment. W.C. Fields, an omnivorous reader, once summed up the uselessness of total recall as a tool for reading when he said that he was probably the only man outside of an insane asylum who remembered all the sub-plots involved in Silas Marner.

In fact, lack of memory is a great help, when one reads for pleasure. It is a real joy to find, in a second-hand store, a book one enjoyed three years ago — but has forgotten. This means one can read the book again, to get a double measure of pleasure out of the same tome.

My grandfather, in fact, always insisted that if one couldn't read a book three times, and enjoy it each time the book wasn't worth buying.

Of course, I realize this view is old-fashioned. Today there is so much to read — instructions on how to build fall-out shelters, tomes outlining how we can all be wiped out in 10 easy ways — that perhaps we need to learn quickly.

After all, the quicker we read it the less it will hurt.

Aug. 30, 1963.

You can't get there from here

There may be a lot of people jumping up and down and cheering about this sort of thing, but personally when I read that in the next five years there will be 1,000 miles of divided, limited access highways built in this part of the country, I break out in a cold sweat.

It isn't that I object to new highways. Is is merely that while they are building the darned things I spend the better part of my motoring life learning the hard way that Ogden Nash was right when he wrote that immortal line:

"You can't get there from here."

To be blunt about the matter, I somehow succeed in getting lost even on old, established highways. A modern clover leaf intersection throws me into a blind panic and on some of those mammoth interchanges I am convinced the highways department should supply drivers like me with a guide. I invariably come out of one of these concrete mazes heading back to where I started from.

So when people construct new highways, and set up detours while doing this, motoring for me becomes a succession of surprises, most of them unpleasant. Once, for instance, I had to drive from New York to my Connecticut home — a 40-mile amble. My wife, when we started, said, "Let's try the new Connecticut Turnpike — I hear it is faster than the Merritt Parkway, and it is getting late."

Three hours later that same wife was saying:

"I certainly do not recall any deer-crossing signs in our neighborhood. Do you know where we are?"

As a matter of fact I did know where we were. We were approximately 215 miles from our Connecticut home, but how we reached that point, or how we were to reverse our plunge into the unknown, I hadn't a clue.

Some people, of course, grow more canny with the years and learn to cope with modern highways, even the detours. But I am not one of them.

The other night, to explain what I mean, I decided to take the family out to our lovely new airport. We would meet some friends arriving there and then eat at the new dining room. My wife, with some justification, questioned the wisdom of this expedition.

"The new highway is going through out there," she said, "and there are some confusing stretches."

But as it was broad daylight I pooh-poohed this, and away we went. In no time the airport was looming ahead of us. Then it was beside us. I turned smartly onto a new road — and the airport began to recede behind us.

I tried again, a flanking approach. I edged up on the airport quietly, so I wouldn't frighten it, and was almost there when the road looped away and once again the airport receded.

As darkness fell, that airport became an even more elusive goal. It was all lit up and stood there, beckoning me, as I approached from the front, the rear and both sides. But the closest I came was when one small road I had hit on petered out at the edge of the tarmac.

"I could race the car right across the airfield," I suggested to my wife, but it was decided that this might be somewhat foolhardy.

Finally a kindly cab driver led us to our destination. By this time, of course, our friends had come and gone. But we did have a lovely meal.

And we also, as my wife pointed out, had a lovely drive in the country.

Mar. 25, 1965.

Time out for planning

The other day I read an article by a management expert who stated categorically that there was no such thing as lack of time — there was only lack of planning.

In other words , the man who complains that he hasn't time to do something is merely admitting that he really hasn't planned his day properly. The way to overcome this, the expert said, was follow some of his simple rules. One such rule seemed so logical, and easy, that I decided to put it into practice immediately.

This rule meant that I would get up a half-hour earlier each working day. A year of such extra half-hours, the expert said, was equal to a whole week of Sundays.

Just why I felt at that time I needed a week of Sundays I do not know. But anyway, the following morning I was up 30 minutes prior to my usual time. My wife, who usually has to physically haul me out of bed in order to get me mobile, immediately wanted to know if I was ill.

I explained what I had read in the expert's article. My wife pointed out that even if I slept there still would be only 52 weeks in a year, and only 52 Sundays, each separated by six days.

By the time we got this family hassle laid away, I was already 15 minutes late leaving for work.

So I tried the same thing the following day. This time everything went well — until the truck in front of me skidded and blocked the road.

Oh well, I could console myself with the knowledge that if I hadn't left for work a half-hour earlier than usual, I would have been 50 minutes late instead of 20.

Another way to make sure you always have time to do what you want to do, according to this expert, is make a list of priorities for each day. Carefully rate them (a, b, c, etc.) in order of importance.

This I did. Under (a) I wrote, "Go to lunch." Then I sat around the rest of the morning wondering what to put in the (b), (c) and (etc.) categories. After all, despite what many people think, I go to lunch only once a day.

The expert also said the busy executive could gain time by handling each piece of paper only once. "When a letter arrives on your desk," he said, "handle it immediately — even if you do nothing more than think about it."

Well, a letter finally arrived at my desk. I immediately picked it up. Then I thought about it.

In fact, I am still thinking about it. But meanwhile, a few dozen other letters have arrived and are quietly gathering dust. Perhaps that expert doesn't get the same kind of mail as I do.

Then it occurred to me. Not only had I not gained a single minute of time by following that expert's advice.

I had actually wasted a lot of time trying to follow his rules. Instead of a 53-week year, as he promised, it looks as though this year will be a 51-week year.

That is, it will be unless I immediately begin to do some work. My own methods may be a trifle untidy and seemingly unplanned, but at least I do get something done occasionally.

Jan. 29, 1972.

Once seen, always forgotten

Quite a few of my newspaper pals seem excited about the fact that there probably will be an election in the near future. But somehow I can't go along with them.

An election, it seems, does nothing but convince me I am the original invisible man.

During election periods, as you know, hopeful candidates prowl about the streets of their would-be ridings eager to "press the flesh" with all and sundry. Which is okay with me, if only the would-be candidate could actually see me.

My encounters go something like this:

Candidate (who has been hastily briefed that I have something to do with the media):

"Hello there Ken Dobson. Know you anyplace. Listen to your program every morning."

I assure him I am not Ken Dobson.

"No, of course not," he agrees. "George Balcan. Good old George. Couldn't start the day without you."

I tell him I am not a radioman. I'm a newspaper columnist.

"Naturally — the old memory misses occasionally. Now I know you. Read you every morning. Really admire the way you always work a chuckle into that column of yours, Mr. Blackman."

I patiently point out that I am not Ted Blackman and I work for an afternoon newspaper.

"You can't fool me. Of course I know you. Look at that

red hair. Hear you have been having a little trouble with the NHL, Red. Look, when I get elected I'll see the right people. It's a shame a fellow gets kicked off TV because of his opinions.

"I'll get you back on the big screen — eh, Red?"

I tell him the confusion flatters me, but no, I am not Red. I write a column three days a week and it appears on the editorial page.

"That's what I thought. The editorial page. Every night after dinner . . ."

The column appears three times a week, I remind him.

"That's what I was saying, every Monday, Wednesday, and Friday night after . . ."

"Every Tuesday, Thursday and Saturday," I reply.

"Just as I was saying, every Tuesday, Thursday and Saturday night after dinner I turn to the editorial page and read your column. I must say you have a keen grasp of politics."

I regretfully say that I seldom write about politics.

"You're on the editorial page and don't write about politics? What in heavens name do you write about?"

That is a bit of a poser. So finally I say I write about everyday things — roses, pretty girls, my wife. But I can see that the candidate's eyes are becoming glazed and he obviously needs help. So I add that I like writing about dogs, too.

"Ah yes, man's best friend. The noble dog. I'm a great supporter of the SPCA, you know. Like to go down there and just stand and look at all those cute dogs."

Finally, it looks as though we have some common ground. But this is an illusion. Actually, we have just reached the real problem.

The candidate has found out what I do. But he doesn't know who I am. So I say, "We've never met before — my name . . ."

"Of course I know you. After reading you all these years I feel you are a personal friend. So long, and don't forget I am a great supporter of the SPCA."

With that he shakes my hand, his assistant stuffs my pockets with campaign literature and he hurries along the street only to turn when he is about a block away to shout, "Support the SPCA."

So I have met the candidate. And the candidate has met me. Although he doesn't know it.

Aug. 24, 1972.

What is needed is more followers

For some time now this present day accent on leadership has been getting me down. Everywhere I looked I read or heard how business firms demanded "leaders." Voters demanded "leaders."

The ads urged: "Be a leader and be a man."

As a fellow who is not too sure that he has the square jaw, charisma and general forcefulness which seem to make up a leader, this was kind of discouraging.

Mind you, I kept telling myself I wanted to be a leader. But even as I said it a childhood memory kept coming back to cause me more than a little unease.

It centred around an occasion, when I was about 10, when I announced to the local gang of mini-ruffians in my neighborhood that I was their leader. "From now on," I announced, "what I say goes."

However, one of this group, a fellow who carried the exotic nickname of "Squirm" decided to debate this announcement.

He debated it so well, in fact, that for about a week I looked out at the world through one eye only. The other refused to function until the swelling had departed.

After that I was cautious about this leadership bit. But, at the same time, I felt guilty about my caution.

After all, who wants to admit that he isn't an embryonic Napoleon or Hoffa?

Now, I am happy to report, these guilt feelings have been banished. In Executives' Digest, a publication prepared for executives, the lead article took exception to the leadership cult.

"What our society needs," the publication stated unequivocally, "is more followers."

The Digest even went on to describe the sterling qualities of a follower. These were outlined in this manner:

"He's the man in the background who makes his leader look good. He's the worker. The leader may order up miracles but it's the effective follower who makes these miracles come true.

"The good follower is intelligent and is able to carry out orders implicitly. He understands and anticipates his leader's ideas and is able to do the job required of him."

How about that, fellow followers? Makes those of us who lack square jaws, charisma and general forcefulness feel pretty good, eh?

Now, when some busybody wants to know why you do not have your name on an office door, not to mention that essential carpet on the floor, you can nod discreetly towards the president's hideaway and say:

"There's my office — he wouldn't be there without me."

Maybe no one will believe you, but at least you will have an answer.

Of course, there is a flaw in this line of reasoning.

Leaders, it seems, always fly first class. Followers go economy. Leaders show up for work in $300 suits. Followers generally look as though they had only recently emerged from a bargain basement melee.

However, if you are willing to overlook these trifles, I am sure there is quite a bit of satisfaction in being a follower, just as the Digest implies.

At least a follower doesn't have to be worried about being beaten up by a fellow called "Squirm."

July 2, 1968.

Fashion nightmare now on the stocks

When President Nixon announced that he planned to visit Mao's China, it was to be expected that the announcement would stir up a lot of discussion.

The Far Righters would cry "sell out." The Far Lefters would claim it was a trick. The majority would probably voice approval because talking is better than fighting.

But one thing I did not expect was the announcement out of New York yesterday which said:

"President Nixon's planned trip to China has spurred American fashion-movers to 'think Chinese'."

In other words, the fashion designers are all ready to deluge us with the New China Look. And somehow the

121

thought of this makes me rather nervous about the future of U.S.A.-China relations.

For instance, in this same announcement there is this statement from fashion guru Billie Donaldson:

"Regardless of whether you like the Communists or not, they've done some perfectly charming things."

I have a hunch if this cute little quote gets repeated in the Red China News, or whatever, a lot of Chinese are going to grit their teeth. It is one thing to absorb a solid, healthy insult. It is something else altogether to be the object of patronizing approval.

But aside from that there are other dangers growing out of this "think Chinese" campaign. As we all know, ever since western women refused to obey the fashion dictators' order to throw away the mini and wear the maxi or the midi, these same fashion dictators have been aching to punish these women.

It could be that this "think Chinese" dictum is not so much political awareness as a chance for the fashion moguls to get even.

At least, the news story I read makes it sound that way.

Already, I am told, designers are at work on Chinese peasant clothes. All North American males need at this point is a world filled with women wearing padded cotton jump suits.

If this does happen, the fashion designers will have achieved what they have aimed at for all these years — a fashion that will make all women look perfectly hideous.

Not only clothes will be involved. Glenn Roberts, director of creative training at Elizabeth Arden, is thinking of an over-all Chinese look. He will, he says, "elongate the eye, pull it out and make it almond-shaped." No, there will be no blood spilled. He claims he will do this with eye-liner and shadow "the color of ancient pottery."

The mind boggles.

But wait, Mr. Roberts is not through with his plans for the new, Chinese woman. He says.

"I see tiny fragile heads with interest in the nape or crown."

Mr. Roberts does not explain what will happen to women who do not have tiny, fragile heads. Does he mean he will revive the ancient art of head shrinking?

And personally, as a long-time girl watcher, I can hardly see myself — or many other males — becoming fascinated by napes and crowns.

But my main worry is political. If this "think Chinese" plot is successful there are going to be an awful lot of frustrated men in America.

As they watch their lovely women disappear under peasant clothing, ancient pottery colors and interesting napes and crowns, they will start to blame it all on Nixon.

"Nixon stay home," will become the slogan. First it will be a murmur, and finally such a roar that there will be a danger that Nixon will stay home.

And pouf — there goes a rare chance for a try at amity. All because fashion designers hate women.

Sept. 2, 1971.

Intimate glimpses into the obvious

Prof. John E. Tropman of the School of Social Work at the University of Michigan, after a study of the relationship of marriage to job mobility among men, has come up with this conclusion:

"Being married almost triples a man's chances for success at work."

This finding did not surprise me at all. In fact, I wondered why anybody had bothered to spend time making a study of something which I thought was obvious to all.

What did surprise me, however, was the fact that Prof. Tropman said he was surprised at his findings.

Come, come professor. You must know that the reason a married man is more successful than a non-married man is that a married man has one great thing going for him that the non-married man hasn't.

Terror. Sheer, unadulterated terror.

Look at it this way, professor. If a non-married critter is passed over for promotion or doesn't get a raise when the other fellows do, he can shrug and forget it.

But not a married man. If a married man does not get the promotion he expects he will never forget about it because his wife will never allow him to forget about it.

So to avoid that kind of thing a married man will do anything — work 18 hours a day, cut the throat of his best friend — to get that promotion.

As for shrugging off the fact he did not get a raise when the others did, well, there is no way that is going to happen to a married man. A few days after the event his wife will say, much too casually, that she has heard everybody at the plant has had a raise.

The married man is caught between two equally distasteful choices. He can lie and say he got a raise. This means he has to give up lunches and the occasional beer with the boys so he can give more money to his wife in order to give substance to the falsehood. Or, he can admit he did not get the raise. Naturally, his wife will not believe him. She will accuse him of holding out on her because she is convinced that extra $10 a week is going to support a mistress.

(Wives, for some reason, always grossly under-estimate the going rate for mistresses.)

In his survey about the success factor of married versus unmarried men, the good professor also discovered that married men are more successful because they are adjustable.

Again, I fail to understand why he was surprised.

The name of the game if a man is to stay married and reasonably sane is adjustability. You all know the dashing writer who was going to get married and spend the rest of his life living in exotic spots where his writing genius would flower properly.

Sure you know him. He's the guy who recently celebrated two great events — his new job as vice-president of that big ad company, and his 25th wedding anniversary.

And during those 25 years the only exotic spot he and his wife have visited is New York. Those business conventions sure do a lot for a happy marriage.

All of which makes me wonder why all this time and money is spent on studies which result in nothing but intimate glimpses into the obvious.

I mean, one other finding the professor made was that married men were less likely to be living a life of crime than the non-married man.

Again, what is surprising about this? Every married man knows how difficult it is to get out of the house on an evening for something as innocent as a poker game.

Think how much more difficult it would be if, when your wife asked: "And where do you think you're going?" you had to reply: "Only down to the corner to knock over the service station."

July 27, 1972.

Statistics will kill us

The news item quoted the coroner as saying the woman drank herself to death. The coroner then added that in his opinion the woman was 108 years old.

This little item seemed to crystalize my feeling that today, in our search for statistics, we are going too far.

We want to know the why and reason for everything and then file it tidily for future reference. We seem unable to accept the fact that some things just happen.

Jean Kerr, author of the delightful Please Don't Eat The Daisies, once told of being taken to hospital. As usual, the hospital had to get facts, facts and more facts before they would even let her in to lie down.

Finally the questioner asked Miss Kerr how old her father was when he died. She said he was 98.

"What did he die of?" was the next question.

Miss Kerr was stunned for a moment. Then she angrily replied:

"He died of being 98, I guess."

It is the same with this old woman in the news item. Surely she is entitled to die at the age of 108 without having to add to some file headed:

"Deaths, Drinking By."

Sometimes, in fact, as I watch these millions and billions of statistics being gathered, I wonder if perhaps they are not being used to mislead us.

I mean, every time some expert wants to make up a report, this expert goes to the files to gather what is euphemistically known as "pertinent statistics."

Then the reports roll out to cause us sleepless nights.

"Juvenile delinquency up 550 per cent in 50 years."

"Cancer 200 times more prevalent today than in 1900."

Anyway, you get the idea. Everything we read and hear is calculated to prove that life is steadily getting worse, and definitely more risky. But perhaps such "facts" should be taken with the proverbial salt. There is that matter of juvenile delinquency, for instance, which is supposed to prove that kids today are worse than kids of 50 years ago.

But are they? Or is that monstrous increase due to the fact that today any misdemeanor, no matter how trivial, gets recorded?

Fifty years ago most kids committing a misdemeanor were sent home to face parental wrath. They may have suffered a bit, but they never became a statistic.

The same could hold true for the terrifying statistics about those dread things that are killing us off at such a rate.

You know, one story says that in the past year 28 per cent of all deaths were due to this, 32 percent were caused by that and another percentage turned up their toes because of something else.

Well, as an experiment, for a month I collected all such published statistics. Then I toted up my own personal file and came to the conclusion that during the past year something like 146 per cent of all Canadians had died — and not one naturally.

Somehow I felt better. I mean, once I realized that I was dead, there seemed nothing else to do but stop worrying and enjoy it.

Sept. 2, 1972.

A guided tour of the fleshpots

Sometimes I think the more permissiveness we have, the less fun we have.

This came to mind because the other day I read one of these uncountable surveys about children and the permissive society.

You know what I mean — whenever there is a dull moment somebody sits down to do an article about the state of sex education amongst the young.

Well, this particular article was a real ambitious effort. It did not look only at the Canadian child or the U.S. child or the North American child.

It took on the problem on a global basis, country by country.

And frankly it was pretty discouraging. Particularly for the young.

For the older folk, mind you, there were some high spots. One country was reported as having a majority of parents who still believe in beating their children.

"I don't mean a cuff on the ear," reported that country's expert on such things. "I mean beating with a stick, or even a board."

As I said, there are still some sensible people in the world.

But what made me happy with the fact that I am no longer a teenager, or a neophyte in sexology, was the dreary, academic approach most experts took to that delightful game known as boy-meets-girl.

One such expert, for instance, solemnly intoned that sex education ought to include intercourse as early as age 13.

But before I could shout "hear hear," he added: "Under teacher's guidance, of course."

Now I ask you, can you think of anything more ridiculous? This man, supposedly an expert, is asking kids who won't even learn math under a teacher's guidance, to have supervised sexual intercourse!

For years now I have been against supervised playgrounds, in the belief that adult supervision inhibits kids and takes away the fun element. It never occurred to me that the next step after supervised midget hockey would be supervised sex.

How would a teacher handle such a situation? Say 2 p.m. every Wednesday was designated on the curriculum for supervised sex.

And every 13-year-old girl begged off because she had a headache?

Also, how do you mark this teacher-guided activity, academically speaking? Is there an "A" for effort? Is there a special award for "the student who shows the most improvement?"

Don't tell me that we are approaching a day when Daddy and Mommy will stand in the auditorium and applaud as Jimmie or Mary walks modestly to the stage to receive the Governor-General's medal for sexual achievement.

Believe me, it is not on prudish grounds that I reject this suggestion that sexual intercourse should be taught with a teacher's guidance.

I am against the whole thing because it strikes me as terribly funny. And because it would take away from kids one of the few non-supervised areas they have left to explore. I still have faith in kids and their ingenuity. Some way, in some manner, a girl knows a boy when she sees one, and vice versa.

As long as that old instinct is there, the kids will do just fine without any guidance from teachers. In fact, guidance might ruin the whole adventure.

Naturally, I have no idea what background the expert who suggested this guidance technique might have. But one thing I do know is that somehow he missed ever being 13 years old.

At that age, if my recall is operating properly, the one thing most 13-year-olds, both male and female, were trying to do was avoid teacher guidance.

Because they wanted to find out what it was all about on their own.

And if I do a kid-count amongst my own generation, I would say we did pretty well without any guidance.

Sept. 28, 1972.

The Rolling Stones gather no praise

Society columnists are fairly unanimous on the point that the birthday party given Mick Jagger and his Rolling Stones recently at New York's St. Regis hotel was the "best party of the year."

So, as I like to keep up with high society, I did a little reading about this great party. It took the form of a supper dance, so I learned.

This supper dance featured a girl who popped out of a giant birthday cake wearing "five pounds of silicone in each breast" — and nothing else.

The entire party engaged in a lemon meringue-throwing bash.

The guests wore jeans, no bras and in many cases no tops.

Perhaps I am old-fashioned, but does this sound like a supper dance to you?

Naturally I realize that social customs have changed. I realize that today it is probably possible to get into the snooty St. Regis wearing a scruffy pair of jeans whereas a few years ago a person so attired would have been hurled into the gutter.

But to go into the St. Regis with no top?

Then there is the matter of the silicone girl popping out of the birthday cake. I understand that this kind of thing used to go on at stags and not-so-nice conventions.

But those kind of parties were usually held in obscure halls, not the St. Regis. And the people attending did not call the society columnists to make sure it was mentioned that they had attended. In fact, the men who did get their names mentioned as attending usually found this information listed in that part of the paper devoted to police news.

But there was no such reticence in this case. Simply everybody was there, from Lee Radziwill to Lord Hesketh to Tennessee Williams.

There was a time I used to think it might be fun to go to a New York Society party. Not that I really believed I ever would. But it was an innocent kind of daydream to wonder what one would say to the society luminaries one read about.

I mean, what did they say to each other and how did they look and how did they behave.

Well, now I know. And somehow I no longer dream about attending such a bash.

It could be that I am stuffy, but somehow I am sure I would be embarrassed if I had to watch a girl, her breasts stuffed with silicone, pop out of a cake.

There is also the matter of dress. Half the fun of a party is dressing up for it. If, instead, I prepared by pulling on a pair of old jeans I would probably never get to the party.

I would, from force of habit, head for the garden and start to weed.

Then there is the way the women dress. I think nudity is fine, but not mass nudity. Wall-to-wall flesh must be somewhat unappetizing because how many really beautiful women and handsome men are there?

As for that pie-throwing bit — it was great in those old Mack Sennett movies but I don't think I would care to take part in that kind of thing myself.

My idea of a supper dance is when you escort a lovely woman who has dressed specially for the occasion and actually dance with her.

You enjoy a delicious meal — not watch it go hurtling through the air — and some pleasant conversation. And you definitely do not have to listen to the Rolling Stones.

This is supposed to be a treat, not a treatment.

However, it would seem that my kind of dance is gone. There is nothing for me to do but go home and listen to my old Artie Shaw and Glenn Miller records.

Aug. 10, 1972.

All that quiver needn't be guilty

A small item in the newspapers recently said that airlines would attempt to combat skyjacking by having their counter personnel take special note of a would-be passenger's "behavior pattern."

The item then went on to say that if a passenger appeared unduly nervous, this passenger would be detained for questioning. But then the item ended. No more information. Which leaves me stranded on the ground, not up in the air.

I mean, if nervousness is the only behavior pattern to be watched for, I guess my flying days are over. After all, any time I am about to be lofted some 35,000 feet above good old terra firma and then hurled through the air at 600 miles an hour, well, let's face it — I'm nervous.

I figure only a damned fool wouldn't be nervous.

Don't get me wrong, I know flying is safe. At least my head knows it, but my stomach doesn't.

It could be that I was introduced to aviation in the wrong way. My first flight, if memory is a reliable guide, was in something known as a Fox Moth.

This was not only the strangest looking aircraft I have ever seen. On the occasion I flew in it the plane was full of fish, freshly caught in a northern lake but growing rapidly older as we droned slowly through the sky.

Since then I have done a lot of flying in everything from the reliable old DC-3 (now, there was a plane) to the latest in jet bombers and passenger planes.

But my stomach has never really agreed with me on this.

That is why I trust the airlines find some other guide-line than merely nervousness to tip them off to a potential skyjacker.

Naturally, I am for anything that will help eliminate sky-jacking. If this means that prior to boarding a plane I have to strip down to my patented drop-seat Stanfields to be searched, fine by me.

But I am sure that nervousness alone will not pin-point aerial bandits. Just the other day, for instance, I had to pick up an airline ticket. I approached the counter and tried to ask for my reservation in a jaunty voice. What came out was a croak.

When I tried to give my air credit card to the girl behind the counter, it slid out of my shaking hand. Those plastic cards are hard to hold in a paw slick with nervous sweat.

Under that new rule, this would have meant instant suspicion.

I have other peculiarities when it comes to flying — all of them destined to draw a dour look from officialdom.

For instance, what would any airline employee think when, after the plane has landed, he sees me hurling little children out of the way and knocking over old ladies as I make a mad dash to the exit?

He would have every right to believe I had some nefarious reason for my frantic plunge. Because how could he pos-sibly know that I am merely so delighted to be back on the ground that I can't wait to get out?

Then there is that annoying, in-flight habit of mine of sitting there clicking my worry beads.

The one consolation I have, if nervousness is to be a barrier to flying, is that if this is so, very few pilots will be able to clutter up the passenger area.

Because the only people who seem more nervous than this writer about flying are pilots. They are rock calm when sitting in the pilot seat. But when their turn comes to ride as passengers, they go all to pieces.

Once, in fact, I was on a flight and the poor fellow next to me was so nervous he kept spilling his martini. I tried to chat with him so as to soothe him.

"What do you do?" I asked. "I'm a pilot," he replied.

At which point I spilled my martini.

Feb. 10, 1972.

Brown paper bags and their uses

Even in this age of frenetic self-improvement, where there are courses on everything from how to improve your posture to how to improve your credit image, I must admit I was a little startled to come across a magazine advertising that it would carry this article:

"How To Improve Your Breathing."

Taking a deep breath, I sat back and tried to figure out just what this might mean. Are some ways of breathing more socially acceptable? Will a good breather get ahead in the world faster than a sloppy breather? Is breathing a key to your personality?

This train of thought intrigued me because up until then I had worried only about waking up some day and finding I had stopped breathing. How I did my breathing had been of no concern to me at all.

Well, occasionally in recent years I have given my breathing some thought. I have wondered, for instance, why steps are steeper than they once were — otherwise, how else can I account for the fact that when I run up a flight of stairs today I puff a little?

But normally, breathing was something that came automatically.

Mind you, I once knew of a man who did have trouble with his breathing habits. It seems that when he became tense, he had a tendency to breathe in gulps of air.

The result was that he got too much oxygen and suffered dizzy spells. In fact, on a couple of occasions he fainted.

His doctor told him he should place a paper bag over his head when he felt tense. Then, when he gulped air, he would gulp a certain amount of carbon dioxide to balance his oxygen intake.

My friend, an advertising executive, followed his doctor's advice. After a tense meeting, he would rush back to his office, close his door, place an ordinary brown paper bag over his head and breathe deeply.

There were slight drawbacks to this, however. One day he felt an attack of tenseness coming on just prior to a meeting and discovered he had left his brown paper bag at home.

Then he spied a discarded bag in the wastebasket. He whipped it over his head, breathed deeply and immediately felt better.

But the meeting he attended was not an unqualified success. It seems the bag he had salvaged had once contained his secretary's breakfast and there he was — sitting at a solemn meeting with bits of sticky Danish pastry adorning his head.

The final blow came late one afternoon. It had been a tough day and my friend, believing that everybody else had left, retired to his office for an un-tensing session.

He was sitting there, head enclosed in a brown paper bag,

when the president, accompanied by an important would-be client, came in.

The first my friend knew of the intrusion was when he heard his president's voice say:

"Mr. Snickle, I would like you to meet our top creative. . . ."

The president's voice kind of trailed off at this point. My friend whipped the bag off his head — but too late. The president and the would-be client were rapidly disappearing down the hall.

"For some reason," my friend said, "we never did get that account. And a few weeks later I left the agency — the president kept looking at me queerly."

As that man was the only person I ever knew who went to the trouble to actually try to improve his breathing, I can hardly wait to read this article, 'How To Improve Your Breathing."

Soon I may find out. .But let me tell you, if that article goes into that bag-over-the-head bit — well, count me out.

My boss is suspicious enough of me already without finding me hiding in a paper bag.

Mar. 31, 1969.

Lester Pearson: the man

Evaluating Lester Pearson as a politician and statesman, and his impact on our country, is a chore I would prefer to leave to more qualified people.

137

But I do think I have some small qualification to evaluate him as a human being.

This thought came to mind as I was excerpting the first book of his memoirs, Mike, for Weekend Magazine.

While the book deals with his early days in the diplomatic service, and stops short of his emergence on the world stage at the United Nations, it is full of typical "Mikeisms."

It could have been a stuffy, self-important book. After all, even in those years Mr. Pearson was a participant in great events.

But, while these events are lucidly explained, Mr. Pearson could not resist the urge to talk about the human side of this diplomatic activity.

So, rightly or wrongly, I stuck to these anecdotes. They show, I think, a young and then-maturing man who worked very hard to promote the interests of his country.

They also show a man who never could take himself too seriously. After the job was done there was always something to chuckle about.

Somehow I feel this is the essential Mike — if I can be forgiven for being so familiar. The man who worked so hard and diligently was also the man who never forgot that a good story at the end of the day helped ease the tensions.

Perhaps one reason I feel this way is due to an experience I had with him during the first Suez crisis.

That was when Britain, France and Israel invaded Egypt to take over the all-important (or so it seemed at that time) canal.

I reported that fracas from the Egyptian side, and spent many an unhappy day out in the Sinai and Gaza strip wondering what the hell was going on. Things were so unsettled that everybody shot at everybody else indiscriminately, and asked for identification later. A situation no sane — and timid — reporter likes.

To tidy up the story I had to fly from Cairo to New York,

and the United Nations, where Mr. Pearson was doing the yeoman work which was to earn him the Nobel Peace Prize.

As Snoopy would write, it was a dark and stormy night when I arrived at Mr. Pearson's hotel headquarters unannounced. But he let me in out of the sleet.

For several hours I sat there and watched as he held impromptu meetings with concerned UN delegates. Then about 1 a.m., he found time to ask what I wanted.

For the next hour or so he patiently answered my questions, although he had been up early the day before. Finally I thanked him, picked up my flight bag and prepared to leave.

Mr. Pearson wanted to know if I had a hotel room. I told him no, but that I would probably be able to get one. He insisted I stay in one of the rooms in his suite because it truly was a dark and stormy night out there.

It was a gesture, I have learned, that few men in his position would make. And I found this same humanity in his book.

Oct. 21, 1972
Weekend Magazine.

Girls that lovely should dance a lot

It is very nice to know that despite the hardships endured during the last decade the Cubans are still the gayest, most fun-loving people in the Western world.

139

At least, that was the opinion I formed during a visit there just after Castro took over. And a recent account of how this warmth and effervescence persists even within the confines of a "voluntary" labor camp seems to show that this opinion is still a valid one.

I must say, though, that my first impression was not such a happy one. Havana's streets, when I arrived, were filled with heavily armed soldiers just down from the hills.

Probably I am overly nervous, but when I look up from my rum punch and find myself peering down the barrel of a submachine gun, I don't feel the urge to chuckle.

But I soon learned that, in this case, appearances were deceiving. These youthful soldiers had been living with their arms for so long in the hills with Castro they automatically kept them within easy reach, even in the city.

The only dangerous moment came about because of an American writer friend of mine, not because of a Cuban. This writer had spent about a year with the Castro forces, and when he bumped into me in a Havana hotel he embraced me like a long lost brother.

About two hours and numerous rum punches later he was calling me a spineless liberal and pushing the muzzle of his gun against my ample middle.

Some Cuban soldiers rescued me. More than that, they restored my equilibrium by inviting me to an impromptu street carnival.

There, in the cool of the evening, the people danced and laughed and insisted that this visitor do the same. And if you haven't danced in the cool of the evening with a beautiful Cuban girl, you haven't danced.

Some time later, as I wanted to find out how the country was taking the transition from Batista to Castro, I took a two-day bus ride from Havana to Santiago.

It was a movable picnic. The bus, at each stop, left off some of its human and animal cargo, and took on a new load of men and women and children and chickens and lambs and, on one occasion, a small, baby donkey.

As the obvious stranger aboard, I was outrageously spoiled.

I was offered food and drinks and everybody was eager to talk to me and never before have the English and Spanish languages taken such a good-natured beating.

Mind you, I am aware that on the occasion of my visit the Cubans were still living with the euphoria of being rid of the bloody Batista. They did not know what might be ahead for them.

But our labor camp article indicates that while conditions may be rough and food scarce, the Cubans still have one thing in abundance. A great love of life.

I really don't know if, when the evening breeze ripples in from the harbor to cool the city, they still have those gay, impromptu street celebrations. For their sake I hope they do.

Girls that lovely should dance a lot.

Jan. 8, 1972.
Weekend Magazine.

Part V

MY WORLD

"You mean you get paid for just making that stuff up out of your head?"

For some years I worked for an editor who obviously felt I needed more experience out there in the great, big world. Every time I returned from an assignment he would welcome me back — but after a few days his urge to further my education would return. He would press some money in my hand and say: "Why don't you go to . . ." Then he would glance at the map on his wall, find a destination and conclude, "Why don't you go there?" Once I asked why he wanted me to go to a particular place and he explained: "Well, it's about 8,000 miles from here."

It is one way to get acquainted with the world.

Paint the town pink

For some reason or other I find it harder and harder to play the role of man-about-town. It is not just that I begin to yawn long before its is midnight — it is also because the town in which I was once a man-about in is changing too fast for me to keep up with.

This fact was brought somewhat brutally to my attention just the other night. My brother-in-law made a quick visit and I decided that we should go out and paint the community at least a decorous pink. So I assumed my jauntiest pose and told him knowingly: "First we'll have a few drinks at this wonderful little bar I know and decide where we will have dinner.

So it was into a cab and away. My brother-in-law seemed properly impressed at being with a sophisticated, knowledgeable man-about-town such as myself and we chatted merrily about the pleasures of living in a big city. Then the cab stopped.

We had pulled up beside a huge excavation. That wonderful little bar, apparently, had served its last drink. But I was undeterred. "There's a place around the corner," I said. "I drop in there quite often."

So in we went. And we had been seated only a few moments when the cigarette girl plunked herself down at our table and exclaimed:

"Frank Lowe — it's been years. Don't you ever go out any more?"

While my wife might have been delighted to hear this unsolicited testimonial to my virtue, I did not think this was giving my brother-in-law the right impression. So I slyly asked her if she didn't think Jimmy's was a nicer place, my plan being of course to imply that I had been doing my man-about-town act of recent years in that bistro. But my loud-mouthed gal cut me short to say:

"Boy, you are out of touch. Jimmy retired a couple of years ago. Now has a home in the country and claims he never wants to see the city again."

I meekly paid my tab and once outside tried to rebuild my image as a gay dog. "There's a roof garden type of place not far from here," I said. "The waitresses, wowee. Black net stockings and all that jazz." And I winked at my brother-in-law and gave him a roguish nudge in the ribs with my elbow.

So up to the roof garden we went. And we were looking at the black net scenery appreciatively when one of the long-limbed beauties leaned over our table, gently pushed my eyeballs back into their sockets, and cooed:

"Mr. Lowe — don't you remember me?"

When I pleaded ignorance, she said: "My mother used to work for you and she took me down to your office a couple of times when I was just a kid."

Well, that did it. I got up and headed for the lobby. When my brother-in-law asked what I intended doing I replied:

"I'm phoning my wife to tell her we'll be home for dinner after all. I find this night-on-the-town business a trifle dull, don't you?"

Oct. 10, 1963.

Tales of naughty suburbs pure fiction

Writers who once sharpened their pens to carve up evil-doers in high places are now all taking dead aim at the modern bacchanalia known as suburbia.

And all I can say, as an old bacchanalia lover from way back is that they should not only give details of what naughty things go on. They should give road maps. My portion of suburbia, unfortunately, would make life in a Sunday school camp look exciting.

All of which is pretty darned frustrating to a guy who has waited all his life to kick up his heels and wink at the pretty girls. Mind you, when the move to suburbia was made, I never mentioned this yen out loud. But I boned up by rereading all the recent epics depicting the joys of moral rot at the end of the rail line, and did a little hoping.

Well, once established on our own grizzled half-acre, I waited eagerly for the call to revelry. Then one day, while hock deep in crab grass, I was approached by a neighbor. He said he was having a little party that night and would I join in.

Will a duck swim? I replied vivaciously, giving him a preview of the wit I would bring to help keep the party going. Then I proceeded to knock together a small wooden cage, explaining that as we hadn't been there long enough to be socially acceptable to the local baby sitters I was whipping up my version of a built-in sitter — a cage for my 7-year-old.

My neighbor laughed gaily and told me to bring the kid along. "But," I expostulated, "at her age she isn't too fond of martinis."

But that is what happened. We went as a closely-knit family, with the exception of daddy. He loped a few yards in front, determined that he was going to get a real good running start at his first suburban wing-ding.

There it was — the patio, the tables, the people. But there was one added ingredient the chroniclers of suburbia in high gear never recorded.

Kids. The place was swarming with kids. I have no statistics to support this statement, but apparently it is illegal to live in suburbia unless one can produce a minimum of six children. And it is also illegal to ever separate them from their parents.

So the jolly evening got underway. I found a tall, frosted glass and took a long, thirsty swallow.

Tell me — how does one get the taste of a butterscotch soda out of one's mouth?

From then on things hit a giddy pace. Hot dogs were devoured, Johnny (6) punched Susie (5) in the snout, and my host bragged that he could down 10 cobs of corn at a single sitting. My grandfather certainly would have been shocked at these modern folk — he was a 15-cob man in his day.

Eventually, emboldened by too much lemonade and feeling appropriately devilish, I edged up to the prettiest woman in the group. Hoisting her baby out of her lap and hanging it on a convenient tree limb, I introduced myself and settled down all prepared to polish up my almost forgotten boy-girl techniques. But before I could think of an opening gambit, she leaned close to me, bathed me in the light of her lovely brown orbs and said:

"You're just the man I'm looking for. Our PTA needs someone to take a school census and . . ."

148

Well, at 10 p.m. our little family was at home. My daughter was persuaded to unlock her cute little hands from around the last two hot dogs extant so she could go to bed. And, feeling almost guilty, I tippy-toed out to the kitchen to open a beer.

I took a swallow (beer doesn't taste the same after butterscotch) and managed to say to no one in particular: "Suburbia — wheeee."

April 12, 1960.

Happy discovery at a today movie

The other afternoon my wife shocked me to the core when she phoned and said she wanted me to take her to a movie that evening.

"Take my wife to a movie?" I queried in unbelieving tones. "Darling, I have too much respect for you. Also, think of my reputation — why, I wouldn't dare be seen in a movie house."

Frankly, I figured I had a pretty good argument. I mean, for the last few years I looked at the ads for movies — and wowee.

After all, I had once seen a skin flick, when I was younger, and almost swore off sex. So what would happen to me today, when I am older and more prone to shock, if I saw a skin flick?

Also, I have been reading reviews.

There was Easy Rider, for instance. As Al Capp said: "The only good thing about that movie was that it had a happy ending — both the lead punks got their heads blown off."

And Midnight Cowboy. People like that I would cross the street to get away from, so who needed to pay money to see them?

So I had sworn off movies. Actually, once I learned how to read a TV schedule, this wasn't very difficult to do.

Because on TV, I discovered, were the movies I used to be hooked on.

Then there was a glorious period — I forget the exact duration — when W.C. Fields returned. I caught up on the Thin Man series — and wasn't Myrna Loy really something? — and another long look at the Marx Brothers.

Fred Astaire and Ginger Rogers took up another entire winter, and then there were visits with Cary Grant and Gary Cooper and Kathryn Hepburn.

So who needed to go down town to see a skin flick?

My wife listened fairly patiently to this argument, but when I had finished merely nodded in the way wives do when they are close to exasperation, and repeated:

"I want you to take me to a movie tonight. There are still good movies, you know."

"Oh no," I recoiled. "You mean we are going to see an art movie? One which is so full of symbols it takes two weeks of talking it over with friends before I realize what it was all about? No thanks."

But my wife was relentless. She insisted there were still movies that even I could understand. Movies which would make me laugh.

"You're kidding," I replied. "All a producer wants to hear in a movie house today is heavy breathing. If he heard a laugh he would cancel the run — he would be sure he had a flop on his hands."

My wife by this time wasn't even listening. She merely told me to meet her at 6:30 p.m., have a drink and then go to a movie. Then she hung up.

It was a very nervous afternoon for me, let me tell you. After something like 10 years I was going to be inside a movie house once again. Would I know how to behave? Would my reactions embarrass my wife? Did I have enough money? I had heard that going to a movie now was about as expensive as taking a trip to Florida.

So I got to our rendezvous earlier than promised. Somehow I had that ominous feeling that this was going to call for more than one drink.

But what do you know? The evening was a smash success.

The movie my wife had dragooned me to happened to be Little Big Man. There I was, front and centre, eyes wide open. The first time I laughed out loud I quickly hushed myself, and looked around nervously.

But I needn't have worried. Everybody else was laughing too.

Imagine that. People in a today movie house sitting there and laughing.

It was was quite a sensation, and quite a discovery.

Who knows, I may go to another movie next year.

Mar. 4, 1971.

A haircut went to my head

As I tried to explain later, there was no way of telling that my regular barber shop had changed hands. So, as usual, I went in, crawled into my regular chair, beckoned to the 80-year-old shoeshine boy and prepared for the usual 15-minute treatment.

Mind you, I had heard these new-fangled barber shops where men had their locks "styled." But such a thing, I thought could never happen to me.

When a fellow has hair like mine growing out of a head like mine — well, nothing much is going to happen. And not in the barber shop where he has been clipped for years and years.

The first indication that things might have changed came when I muttered, "the same, Mike — scissors on the side and no smelly tonic," and heard a voice say:

"I'm Angelo, and you really should do something with your hair."

Lifting my baby blue eyes from the girlie magazine I was perusing I gazed into the lustrous brown eyes of Angelo. Already Angelo was grasping my wispy locks, shaking his head in horror and saying:

"Oh my yes, something must be done. Nobody has hair like this."

I was a little intimidated. For the first time it struck me maybe there was something wrong with my hair. Up to this moment I had been quite satisfied with it — it kept my skull warm and on most occasions stayed out of my eyes. What else could anyone expect from his hair?

But Angelo obviously wasn't very happy about me or my hair. And as he kept waving a razor in one hand as he talked I told him to go ahead. "Nobody could do anything with this head of hair anyway," I said letting my eyes stray back to the girlie magazine.

Forty-five minutes later, after I had finished my third girlie magazine, Angelo swung me around to face the mirror. "Look," he said, "the new you, by Angelo."

I looked. "Migawd," I screamed, "Hitler is alive and is a fat-faced blond."

Then I looked again. It wasn't Hitler. It was me. A me with a blonde cowlick.

Angelo was ecstatic. "If only you had better hair," he said, "I could make you pretty."

But I wasn't so sure. For years I had been running a damp comb over my cranium to pull my hair back in the least tiresome and most tidy fashion. And now, with my hair trimmed and shaped and shortened and pulled down over, not back from, my forehead I had to return to my office and give my colleagues a look.

"Angelo," I whispered as I nervously prepared to leave, "if this doesn't work I am going to re-style your face."

I crept into my office but before I could get to my own cubby hole and hide behind the closed door, my secretary spotted me.

"Oh," she ohed. "You've had your hair styled."

"Wait until the boys back in the poolroom in Bible Hill hear that," I thought as I kept trying to creep behind my office door.

But then my secretary cried: "Girls, come and look. Mr. Lowe has had his hair styled. He looks great."

I paused in my tracks. "Looks great" she said? At least that's what I heard.

So I decided to try out Angelo's handiwork on my greatest critic. My daughter. I went home and threw my new head into the living room.

"That's swift," my daughter said. "Real swift."

I preened. Then she said, "If you'd just lose 30 pounds — boy, you'd be handsome."

May 16, 1968.

Gloom keeps them happy

It had been so many years since I had had an honest-to-goodness vacation, it seemed on this one I had forgotten the ground rules. In fact, during the first days of this vacation I began to notice that something was wrong.

Not with me, I might hasten to add. I was going about my vacation duties of swimming twice a day, eating wonderful meals, enjoying my afternoon snooze, just as though I had a vacation every year.

It was the family that let me down. The wider I smiled, the louder I hummed, the longer I slept, the more joyously I bounced in those long, bubbly Atlantic breakers — the more glum my daughter and wife became.

At first I couldn't understand it. I tried to get things jolly all around by drawing attention to our accommodations (first class), the ocean (five miles of beach with a rolling surf), the weather (never below 80 degrees in the daytime), the meals (lobster, clam chowder, 10-minute-old corn).

"Enjoy, enjoy," I carolled as I took another belt of U.S. gin which costs a heck of a lot less than the Canadian equivalent. "It is a wonderful vacation."

But my efforts were in vain. The happier I became, the more glum my wife and daughter looked.

Then, one evening as I sat and watched those who had gotten weary and sweaty walking 100 feet up from the ocean plunge into the hotel pool, the answer came to me. I was violating the basic ground rules for a happy family vacation.

I was indicating that I was enjoying myself.

This is a fundamental error on Good Old Dad's part. Because the minute he indicated that he likes the accommodations, enjoys the food and is generally enjoying his vacation, his wife and child become suspicious.

They immediately suspect that he is happy because the vacation is not really an expensive one. He is happy because he has installed them in a cut-rate joint and everyone else they know is living much better.

If he is so gosh-darned happy, the wife and daughter figure, he can't be worried. And if he isn't worried he isn't being a good husband and father. He is not paying enough for his vacation.

As I said, this realization came to me just in the nick of time. Another day, I am sure, and my wife and daughter would have rebelled and decided to change the entire vacation plan. My enjoyment had them really edgy and upset, let me tell you.

Fortunately, though, just before they could launch their revamped vacation plan, I remembered what I had to do. After that I stopped smiling. I stopped humming. And one very effective gambit was to interrupt my sleep — and theirs, too — with great shrieks of undiluted terror.

This did it. In a couple of days, as I became glummer and my nightmares more violent, my wife and daughter bloomed and beamed. The world was normal again. Good Old Dad was worried sick so they must be in the best of all possible places.

So I continued to swim twice a day in the long, bubbly Atlantic breakers, eat wonderful meals, take my afternoon snooze and consume the occasional belt of that under-priced U.S. booze. It was, indeed, a wonderful vacation.

But I never let on to my wife and daughter that it was a wonderful vacation. If I had, they would have had a miserable time.

Sept. 6, 1966.

The face is familiar but . . .

The other night, just before I fell asleep, I made a mental note to call Doug first thing in the morning. Then I sighed, snuggled deeper into the bed when, whammo, I could not think of Doug's last name.

"This is silly," I told myself, "I see Doug three or four times a week. I've known him years. Now let's see, his last name is . . .?"

The name would not come. By this time I was wide awake, what is left of my little mind darting and twisting as it attempted to unlock the memory capsule containing Doug's last name.

I tried going through the alphabet, thinking of all the surnames I knew beginning with "a," then all the surnames beginning with "b," and "c," and "d." I finally came to "z" at approximately 2:30 a.m. and by this time, although I was no closer to remembering good old Doug's last name, I was further from sleep than ever.

"This is nonsense," I told myself firmly. "I'll forget all about it until the morning. Then, if I still can't remember the name, my secretary will know it."

But that was no good. Obviously I was not going to sleep without first remembering Doug's name. So I stared into the dark and recalled Doug's face, his job, his wife, his dog, his favorite drink, his voice. The only thing I could not recall was his last name.

"Think about something else," I commanded myself sternly, "and then it will come to you — just like that." When I said "just like that" to myself I automatically snapped my fingers and the dog came rustling in carrying his leash in his mouth.

The night, or what was left of it, was getting out of hand.

After I got rid of the dog I began to think about something else, as I had told myself to do. But all I could think of was names. I remembered in Grade II there was a kid sitting behind me called Parkington Worth. The first girl I ever took out was called Greta Gunn. The name of my first teacher was Miss Fallis.

But I still could not think of Doug's last name, even though I had seen Doug the previous day.

The night wore on. I remembered vacations at Tatamagouche, swimming at Ecum Secum bridge. I learned I could recall the names of the 10 provinces, two territories and the 50 states. I remembered the name of the first horse I ever bet on — Darky Gratton — and the name of a girl I had talked with for only two hours almost 22 years ago — Wendy MacPherson.

But I could not remember Doug's last name.

Finally I could stand it no longer. Even though I realize that waking my wife up before she has had her eight solid hours of sleep is almost as foolhardy as kicking a tiger on the nose, I shook her until she muttered, "uummph, whassat — what time is it?"

"It's early yet," I said. "But darling, can you tell me Doug Donnelly's last . . ."

"Whassat you said?" she asked, still not awake. "whattayawant?"

"Never mind, dear," I said wearily. "It was all a mistake." And I rolled over and went to sleep.

July 28, 1964.

Write and wrong

It is a painful thing to face up to, but I finally have to admit that my niche in life — at least from an outsider's viewpoint — is an extremely minor one. I mean, people seem to constantly make remarks which indicate that they don't think writing is really a very honorable, or arduous, way to make a living.

This started some time ago. A secretary I had at that time watched her new lord and master (me) for a few weeks and then asked:

"You mean you get paid for just making stuff up out of your head?"

When I assured her that this was the case she didn't seem at all impressed. Instead she muttered:

"Geez, what a soft touch."

Well, I figured she was young and unknowing so I passed this off. After all, no man can be a hero to his secretary. But gradually I began to notice that this secretary was not alone in her beliefs about what I did.

A little while ago, for instance, my wife was talking to an acquaintance. This woman tried to be nice by saying that she wouldn't miss reading my stuff. Then she asked my wife:

"Tell me, is your husband amusing when he is at home?"

My wife looked a little startled but rallied to reply:

"Of course. He's a barrel of laughs around the house."

Her acquaintance thought this over for a moment and then said:

"That must be nice. My husband never says anything

amusing. But then, he has a very important job."

A remark like that can set a fellow thinking, believe me.

There are other indications that my kind of work is not exactly equated as being on the same status level as, say, a nuclear physicist. Just the other night a group of men were questioning me about the writing "game" when one said.

"Yeah, I guess it can be a bit of a chore. But then, you're not a real writer like those fellows who have to put names in their columns. You know, those gossip column fellows who have to tell us what is going on."

It can really do something to a man's ego, not to mention his id, to realize that in the human scale he is rated as lower than a gossip columnist.

But apparently it is something which must be lived with. Even my own relatives aren't immune (far from it) to taking a whack at my way of life. Not so long ago one dear relative was talking about his daughter. "A bright girl, did well in college, majored in English Literature but hasn't made up her mind what to do in life."

Wanting to show that I was all for family solidarity I said: "Perhaps she'd like to try her hand at newspaper work . . ."

And that was as far as I got. The proud father shouted: "My daughter? In newspaper work? A writer? Why . . ."

But I cut him off at the blasphemy. Obviously he was not impressed by my attempt to offer help.

Even my own mother has done little to show faith in what I do. She still asks me when I am going to settle down and when I ask her what she means she sighs and says:

"Well, I think it is nice for a man to write as a hobby — but what do you do for a living?"

Mar. 10, 1966.

A tip of the hat to Frank Sinatra

It is probably heresy for a newspaperman to say this, but I really felt sorry when I read that Frank Sinatra had finally quit show business.

I say this is probably heresy because Frank Sinatra had no love for newspapermen. And this feeling was reciprocated, believe me.

In fact, I once had an editor who flatly refused to have a Frank Sinatra article in his paper. Unless, of course, it was a derogatory one.

Heaven knows, there were enough of those. Sinatra was continually getting into brawls, accused of being mixed up with hoods and figuring in drinking scenes.

But despite that, he had one over-riding gift. He was an honest performer. He had a great respect for his audience and a tremendous pride in his work. Which means that the audience usually got its money's worth.

This, unfortunately, cannot be said of all performers. Particularly some performers after they have achieved what is known as star status.

Quite often, after attaining this giddy eminence, they try to ride on the name alone. The result can often come close to grand larceny as the audience puts up its money — and gets a ho-hum, couldn't care less kind of performance.

This does not mean that all Sinatra performances were great. Some of his movies, in fact, were plain lousy. But when it came to his live performances, and his records which

160

were to go on sale, he really tried to give his best.

Once, I recall, in New York he came on stage to face the usual packed house. Whatever he had been doing prior to the show, he hadn't been practicing, that's for sure.

In fact, he was looped.

Some stars, under such circumstances, would have tried to fake it. But Sinatra, after a few false starts, apologized. The rest of the show went on and during this time I don't know what kind of a purging he went through back stage. But eventually he reappeared.

He grinned, apologized again and said if the people would like to hang around he would do his best to entertain them. And that was a show, my friends. He took that audience, a sullen group who were sure they had been gypped, and belted them with every ounce of his talent.

He also gave them twice as much as originally scheduled. It was a great night with an honest performer.

I never met Sinatra, nor even interviewed him. So I can't speak from personal experience. People I did know who had been or were close to him, however, came up with almost identical comments.

He could be nasty, apparently, for no other reason than he happened to feel nasty at that moment. Contrarily, he could be most considerate and generous — sometimes to the very same people he had previously treated badly.

He was moody, a fellow who preferred to stay up all night. But, nobody ever knocked his professionalism.

Even I got a chance to verify that. I was doing an article once about how a recording is made. In the studio that day was Sinatra.

I watched, fascinated, as he worked and worked and worked. Over and over again. Finally, when he was dripping with sweat, the director said the final version was okay so let's play it.

Sinatra and the band and entire crew listened. At the end

everybody crowded around and said things like "beautiful" and "great". Even the man in charge said: "That sounds good to me."

Sinatra snarled: "To me it sounds like Frank Sinatra with a cold. Let's try it again."

So back to the grind.

As I said, I know nothing about what he was like as a person. But that kind of professionalism I can admire.

So I, for one, will miss him.

Mar.25, 1971.

Manifestations of affluence

While it is popular these days to talk about affluence, and the benefits and evils thereof, in my little crowd the term "affluence" is seldom used. Instead, we tend to talk about that other mid-20th century economic barometer — that thing known as "the poverty level."

None of us is really sure just what the poverty level might be, but all of us are convinced that we have been living in that unfashionable neighborhood for quite some time. So it is a bit of a game to try to explain when you first realized you had climbed above the poverty level.

One man, for instance, said he first realized he had moved into new economic strata when he discovered he could afford to wear a clean shirt each and every day. Another friend said the great moment arrived for him when he realized he could take a taxi without feeling guilty about the expense. And a third opined that he had crossed the

Great Divide the day he bought a bottle of booze and got home to discover he really didn't need it — there was still half-a-bottle in the house.

Mind you, none of these friends of mine talk about affluence, whatever that may be. They are merely delighted to find that at some point they made the happy discovery that the wolf was no longer actually on the doorstep. He still might be wandering around in the area, but for the time being he wasn't breathing through the keyhole.

While I enjoyed these little discussions, and was very happy for my friends when they recounted their own moments of economic truth, I always felt kind of out of it. Try as I might, I couldn't recall a single moment when I felt I, too, had inched my way above the bare subsistence level.

True, I had reached the point where I could wear a clean shirt each day. But I still felt guilty about buying shirts. I took taxis, but was always convinced that some day that Great Bookkeeper in the Sky would call me on this. As for having more booze in the house than I needed — well, my conscience never did adjust.

At least, that was the state of my economic id up until last Saturday when I went shopping for some spring garden necessities. When I got home my wife casually asked what I had bought. I detailed the stuff and finally, and very hesitantly, added:

"And I also bought a wheelbarrow. It's only a small wheelbarrow and it only cost $11. I know it was silly of me, with the little bit of gardening I do, but I couldn't resist. It's green and yellow and, well, I've always wanted to have a wheelbarrow."

My wife took this very casually and said she hoped that my wheelbarrow and I would have a long and happy life together. "If you want a wheelbarrow," she said, "you deserve to have one."

163

It was one of those small, genuinely happy moments a man can have. I sat in the living room and re-lived the entire experience.

I had gone into the store and ordered the fertilizer for the lawn. Then I bought some rose food. And peat moss and grass seed.

Then, as I was walking over to pay the bill, I saw the wheelbarrow. For years now, I have wanted one. It seemed to me it would be the height of luxury to start out for a morning's gardening with everything one needs piled neatly into a wheelbarrow and not have to continuously walk from the garden to the garage or, worse still, try to carry everything in one's arms.

So without a pause — I didn't even think about the mortgage or whether or not my child had shoes — I pointed at the wheelbarrow and said: "I'll take that, too."

I didn't even ask how much it was.

And as I sat and relished this great economic breakthrough I was hugging to myself another bit of information which was additional proof that I had reached some kind of plateau. You see, at the very moment I bought the wheelbarrow I also saw a spade I had always wanted. I ordered it, too, even though I have a perfectly good shovel.

If that isn't climbing above the poverty level I don't know what is.

April 29, 1969.

164

Varying views on punctuality

The ideal mate, most women seem to believe, would be a stop-watch.

A man can be a slope-headed bore, with all the charm of a two-toed sloth, but if he gets home each night at 5:33 p.m. precisely, never a minute earlier nor a minute later, he is obviously as desirable a mate as a desert sheik who spends his time trying to remember how many oil wells he has.

At least, all the other wives in the area sigh about this walking metronome and hold him up as "a good example."

"You can set your watch by George," they explain with admiration lending warmth to their voices. "Not like some people I know."

The last statement, of course, is designed to make you-know-who squirm with guilt. Because you-know-who has never turned up on his own doorstep at the same time on two consecutive evenings during all his married life.

And, despite good old George, suburbia's answer to automation, you-know-who has no intention of doing so in the future.

First, let's look at George's side of it. Every morning he leaves his house at 8:27, checks into his office at nine and leaves precisely at five — to get back to his nest in time to molt at 5:33. A well-trained laboratory mouse can do the same.

There is also the question of why a woman finds this

mechanical approach to marriage so laudatory. Is she so insecure about George — a man, I bet, who would be safe alone on an island with 100 girls — that she hits the panic button if she doesn't see him loom in the doorway at the expected time? Or, and this is probably closer to the truth, has she so little faith in his ability to find his way home that if he is two minutes late she envisions him lost forever?

The wives' view of this, however, is a little different. They claim that George's rigid comings-and-goings prove that he is devoted and reliable. These are fine adjectives when applied to a horse or a dog, but shouldn't a husband represent a little more to his wife than that?

After all, it is common knowledge that a wife gets bored very easily these days. And once she gets bored she is liable to do all sorts of foolish, marriage-wrecking things — such as joining a bridge club or rushing out to take a job.

Therefore, it is the duty of every marriage-cherishing husband to keep his frau on her toes, shake her out of her rut, make her so mad she won't have time to be bored. And what better way than to be a little irregular in your homecoming hours?

It doesn't cost anything unless someone is rude enough to count the cost of the stop at the local sarsaparilla parlor, and it doesn't take much ingenuity — at least I find that getting home late is one of the things I do easiest and best.

Other men may brag about their cocktail formulas, old George may smugly hold onto his reputation as the neighborhood mechanical man, but I can brag about keeping 'em guessing. Not just my wife, either. The neighborhood wives, who ordinarily wouldn't waste a second glance on a tubby, nondescript like me, have made me something of a local celebrity.

When I leave the house there is an excited buzzing about my probable hour of return. My wife claims bitterly that they run a neighborhood pool on this, but I modestly insist that she shouldn't brag about me this way.

If this keeps up, in fact, old George is going to have to work hard at retaining his place in the suburban sun.

He may still be the "ideal husband," from a wife's point of view, but can any other husband but me say that when he sets off for work he is carrying on his nose the pin money of every woman on the block?

It kind of makes a fellow feel proud.

May 31, 1969.

Those games that people play

One of the more dangerous social games a man can play, apparently, is not spin-the-bottle nor post office. In those games the worst that can happen is that a guy may get kissed.

The game I am talking about can earn you a punch on the nose.

This game doesn't have any real name, as far as I know, but it might be called, "Do You Remember Old What's His Name?"

It occurs when you unexpectedly bump into someone from your old home town.

This bumpee completely ignores the fact that you left your old home town while a stripling in your teens, and have returned since then only for quick visits.

He also assumes that you have complete and instant recall.

Your first warning that you are once again to play, "Do

You Remember Old What's His Name?" usually is a slap on the back in a hotel lobby and a loud voice saying:

"Frank, old boy — how are you?"

You turn, to stare into a completely unknown face.

But once you *have* turned, you are trapped in the game. The first few moves, however, are not too painful. You merely paste a fake, gee-it's-great-to-see-you-old-buddy smile on your face, and hope this inquisition won't last too long.

That hope is soon gone. You try to say you are busy but he grabs you by the arm and insists you sit awhile and talk about the old home town. And as everybody I grew up with in my old home town got to be at least six feet tall, while I never topped the five-foot-six mark, I generally find myself doing just this.

Then the game begins in earnest.

"Remember Jack Brimsley," your antagonist asks.

"Jack Brimsley?" you mutter.

"Sure, good old Jack," he adds. "Used to take out your sister."

"Oh, you mean the guy with the squint?" you parry.

"No, no," is the reply. "Great big fellow. You must remember him. He once gave you a real licking for spying on him when he was courting your sister in the parlor."

"Oh, yeah," you laugh hollowly. "Good old Jack Brimsley."

"I knew you'd remember Jack," your unknown boyhood buddy goes on. "He finally married Ruth Flam — you remember Ruthie?"

"Ruth Flam?" you query. "A big, sloppy girl?"

The hand on your arm tightens painfully. "Watch it, old buddy," your old buddy growls. "Ruth Flam is my sister-in-law and a sweeter, lovelier girl you never met."

"Sure, sure, old buddy," you whimper. Just take it easy on my arm — that's my drinking arm you're holding."

All this time, of course, you are not only completely in

the dark about these people he is mentioning; you are just as completely in the dark as to who your old buddy might be. So you try your own inept hand at gamesmanship.

"You were quite a cut-up in the physics lab," you say, remembering that there had been a large, beefy lad whose name you could not recall after all these years who had been such a character.

"No," he replies. "You're confused. You're thinking of the biology classes. Boy, what a ball we had."

However, as you had been turfed out of the biology class on grounds of gross stupidity after the first couple of sessions, this doesn't help in the identity hunt.

But your old buddy goes on. "You must remember Doris Timbo," he says. "You took her out enough times."

This time the memory machine does work. You whistle and, happy to at last show some signs of intelligence, say something like:

"Boy, was she a hot number. Wowee. Do I remember Doris . . ."

It is at this point that one is liable to receive the punch on the nose. Because Doris Timbo, naturally, is this guy's sister. And this guy — all too belatedly you remember — is Dick Timbo, once our school's best all-round athlete.

The only time I ever played this game, and enjoyed it, in fact, was when a fellow greeted me and after we went over a list of names, all unknown to me, he said: "Aren't you Frank Smith from Ecum Secum?"

That's the way all these meetings should end.

Aug. 5, 1969.

Distant drumming heard in a kitchen

Women will never believe this, but the reason men shun kitchen chores is that they know it is against nature — they know that a man has no place in a kitchen.

They also know that when a man goes against nature, retribution is bound to follow.

As I said, women will scoff at this explanation. They claim men shun the kitchen because they are too lazy to help out with household chores.

But over the years I have accumulated a lot of evidence to prove that any man who ventures anywhere near a kitchen is violating some kind of natural law — and he should beware.

Consider what happened to a friend of mine only last week, for instance.

My friend's wife was ill, so he stayed home to keep the house running.

"I swear I could hear those voodoo drums warming up the minute I went into the kitchen," he recalled later, when he came out of shock. "But I tried to put this down to imagination."

Anyway, the first thing he had to do was to get some things out of the refrigerator. And during this macabre tale you should realize that this man is living in a nice new apartment, equipped with nothing but the newest and best in the way of kitchen machinery.

He dug into the refrigerator's innards and came up with

what he thought he needed. He straightened up and whammo — his head came into sharp and agonizing contact with the door of the freezing compartment.

"I swear I never opened that door," my friend told me. "That Unseen Hand which punishes husbands who venture into kitchens must have opened it."

However, the cut on his head was not very bad, merely messy. You know how those scalp wounds bleed.

Some time later my friend decided to wash up some dishes. He stacked all the dirty dishes into the spanking new, automatic dishwashing machine, set all the proper dials and then went into his den to read.

"Sometime later," he told me, "I decided to get a drink. So I went into the kitchen — and immediately was up to my ankles in boiling water."

The spanking new, automatic dishwasher had decided to go on the fritz. Water, boiling hot water, was gushing from it like hot lava from a minor volcano.

"Have you," my friend asked me, "ever gotten down on your hands and knees in boiling hot water to search for a valve under the sink so you could turn off your dishwasher?"

This episode cost him some minor burns and one more small gash on the skull — caused by said skull coming into contact with a hitherto hidden pipe under the sink.

"By the time I got the water slopped up and assured the neighbors below me that I had no intention of flooding them out, I noticed that those vodoo drums were sounding much louder," he said.

"But it was too late to turn back. I had promised the doctor my wife would not be disturbed and there was still the problem of dinner coming up."

My friend thought he had this dinner business well in hand. His instructions were straightforward enough. He was to put the roast in the oven at 4:30 p.m., turn the thermostat to 300 and in an hour or so a female neighbor was to arrive to look after the complicated business of getting the vegetables ready.

"I did exactly as I had been told," my friend said. "The only trouble was that as I turned the thermostat on our new stove the entire contraption came away in my hand.

"There I was with a handful of dial, wire and bolts and I didn't know what temperature the oven might be at."

"What did you do then?" I queried.

"I was very cool and collected," my friend said. "I carefully opened the kitchen window and threw the thermostat out. Then I carefully opened the dishwashing machine and just as carefully threw out every dish in the thing.

"Then I carefully dialed the phone and arranged to have a woman come in by the day. And then I carefully mixed the biggest martini you ever saw and retired to my den.

"That's where a husband belongs."

"Amen," I said, "No husband should go against nature by venturing into a kitchen."

Mar. 15, 1969.

Sound and fury all for nought

As I looked at all those Canadian flags snapping in the breeze or drooping in the rain this past weekend, I wondered where all the fury had gone.

Remember when the then Prime Minister Pearson introduced the "Pearson Pennant?" Come on, of course you do.

At the time I couldn't understand what the uproar was all about. In the world in which I grew up, the maple leaf had always been Canada's most distinctive symbol.

Without giving it a second thought we had instinctively turned to the maple leaf when we most needed an easily recognizable symbol — during World War II.

At that time, maple leaf symbols appeared on the funnels of our war ships, on the sides of our bombers and on direction signs leading to army positions.

Why, I asked myself, would it be wrong to make the maple leaf our official symbol and put it on a flag we could call our own?

Which showed how naive I was. To test reaction, while the debate about the flag raged on, I had a copy of the proposed new emblem specially made.

One quiet, sunny Sunday afternoon this strange new device was hoisted on my front lawn. I sat quietly in a deck chair nearby to see what would happen.

Word of the new flag spread rapidly. First the neighbors came to look and comment. Then cars began cruising by, slowing down to let the riders have a look. Quite a few stopped to allow the riders to express their views.

Through all this I sat quietly, pretending I was reading and not saying a word. Part of this was because I wanted to hear what other people had to say — but part of it was sheer cowardice.

I had no intention of admitting I was the traitor who had run up this particular banner.

I was particularly terrorized by a trio of little old ladies. These women made no bones about what they would do to the person who had put up this particular flag, if only they could get their hands on the rascal.

The most common misconception at that time was that the former Canadian flag, the modified Red Duster, had led our troops into battle in two world wars and to think of another flag was to insult the memory of the men who had fought.

I would have liked to have told these people that this was not the case, but as much as I like to be the centre of attention, something told me that day to keep quiet.

Anyway, after taking my own, unofficial poll, my admiration for Mr. Pearson's courage grew.

I was challenging the beliefs of only a few. He was taking on — or so it seemed at the time — an entire nation.

In retrospect, of course, this commotion seems somewhat ridiculous. Our maple leaf is known and respected everywhere, even here in Canada.

Kids plaster the maple leaf on their packsacks as they hitch through foreign countries — they seem to feel that it will immediately identify them as Canadians and so ensure them better treatment.

Businessmen junketing abroad wear maple leaf pins for the same reason and motorists in foreign lands slap maple leaf stickers on their autos.

Some people claim that American tourists in Europe, at least some of them, are using the maple leaf emblem, too — in hopes they will "pass" as Canadians.

I guess Mike Pearson knew what he was doing after all.

July 4, 1972.

My life-long battle with the telephone

One good thing about being president of the United States, or so I think, is that obviously one is always assured of getting a phone call through.

You know what I mean. When astronauts come back from the moon, they are barely out of their capsule before the phone rings and President Nixon is chirping away with his congratulations.

Frankly, this is one of the main points I admire about President Nixon — his ability to get a telephone call through at the right time.

Naturally, I have no way of knowing what your batting average is when it comes to telephone calls. But mine is not really big league — certainly a dismally far cry from the president's 1,000 average.

It could be that I was not emotionally prepared to be a skilful man with a phone. I mean, when I was a child living in a small and not very sophisticated community, even a telegram was still regarded with suspicion.

So with this background people such as my grandfather and grandmother regarded the telephone with a great deal of suspicion indeed. If a telegram was bad news, hearing the long distance operator say "This is a long distance call" was enough to give my grandmother cardiac arrest.

As soon as she heard those dread words, she would drop the receiver and run for my mother, shouting, "It's long distance, it's long distance."

175

I don't recall what she expected my mother to do, but I do remember viewing these scenes with rapt attention — and perhaps right at that time beginning to feel that the telephone was not an instrument to be regarded lightly.

Even as a teenager, at that moment in life when the telephone is supposed to be an extension of one's ear, I never had the chance to get real matey with that electronic gadget.

First of all, when you are on a party line, you are not encouraged to use the phone for idle chatter. If you do, some irate housewife along the line is apt to give you an earful.

Also, while teenagers today spend hours on the phone exchanging intimate secrets, a teenager with nothing but a party line at his disposal had no such inclination — not if he wanted any of his secrets to remain secret, that is.

In fact, I can remember walking a couple of miles merely to ask a girl for a date. If I had used the phone to ask her, and she turned me down, I would be publicly shamed and labelled for life as an unsuccessful would-be Romeo.

So when I got to the age where the phone became a business rather than a social necessity, I guess I simply wasn't psychologically equiped to handle it.

Unlike President Nixon, when I make a call the person I want to talk to does not immediately materialize on the other end of the line. Instead, somebody will ask who is calling.

Then, when I give my name, there is a whispered conversation and eventually I am told that the person I wish to talk to is hunting for fossils in the Gobi Desert and won't be available for the next two years.

I bet that never happens to President Nixon.

In the last few years, of course, I have not only had my psychological shortcomings to contend with when it comes to the phone, I have had the phone company itself.

When I place a long distance call, for instance, a disapproving voice chastises me for not knowing the area code. And I bet that has never happened to President Nixon, either.

July 29, 1971.

Time to exercise caution

This is the time of year — the first unbroken week of work after the festive season — when an employee must act with extreme caution.

Because this is the week the bosses are trying to keep all those resolutions they made in the ghastly dawn of January 1.

And boy, are they mean.

A typical "this week" kind of thing is that ordinarily routine Monday morning meeting. Usually it is quite a casual affair at 9 a.m., designed to set some direction for the week's work.

But this week it was different. The boss, instead of slouching in an easy chair, was sitting at attention behind his desk. His opening words were:

"From now on we should have this meeting at 8:30 a.m. — give us an extra half-hour."

The uninitiated might be inclined to argue this dictum. But not the old pros. They merely chorus, "Great idea, boss."

They know that somehow the boss, when his eyes opened on that fateful January 1, had decided to tighten things up at the office. They also know the 8:30 dictate will not last very long.

Then there is the boss who ducks into your office about 10 a.m. "Nice little place you have here," he comments. "Out of the way, private."

"Yes," you agree. "That's why it is affectionately known as 'the dungeon'. Look at that wonderful view out there. Did you ever see such glorious bricks?"

But he isn't listening. He is staring at the pack of cigarettes on your desk.

"Still smoking, eh?" he asks. "Well, you're lucky to have an office like this. No one can see you so no one would know if you were smoking or not. Would they?"

You agree that no one would know. And with a great feeling of compassion you silently offer him a cigarette.

Because this boss has publicly quit smoking as of about 6 a.m. January 1. It isn't his fault that his office is big and open and generally filled with nosy people. So who are you to make cracks about his sitting in your little hideaway sneaking an illicit smoke? Especially when you know that such cracks would be the same as asking for a pink slip.

This week also presents a lunch problem. There is bound to be the boss who insists on taking you to lunch.

You get seated and with a great show of false jollity he says: "Well, how about some carrot juice and a bowl of lettuce? That should hit the spot."

You agree, but remembering that this is your week to be cautious you don't specify the exact spot carrot juice and a bowl of lettuce might hit. After all, it is already January 8, and with any luck by January 15 this boss will be back on his roast beef routine.

An even greater hazard, of course, is the boss who has decided that 1969 will be his year for combining dieting with greater efficiency. He is the one who announces at noon that he is giving up his lunch hour.

"I'll mix a raw egg with a glass of milk," he explains while his staff turn slightly green, "and after drinking that I'll have the entire lunch hour for work. No one around, no phones ringing — it will be great."

The one consolation in all this, naturally, is that bosses are human. Well, they have human lapses.

And one human lapse is that they will no more be capable of holding on to these new and pure modes of living than any of us would be. In another week or so things will be back to normal.

But until then my only advice to young and inexperienced employees is to exercise extreme caution. A hungry, smoke-less, dehydrated and hard-working boss is a treacherous thing to have to live with.

Jan. 9, 1969.

Don't regret a thing, mom

Dear Mother:

For many years now, I realize, you have been berating yourself for not having been able to send me, your only son, to college.

Many times you have mentioned this to me, implying that if you had been able to send me to college perhaps life would have been easier for me — even if it would have been almost impossible for you at the time.

But now I can assure you that you need nurse this regret no longer. It seems to me that by not being able to finance

179

your boy through college you saved him from an unimaginable fate.

I mean, surely you wouldn't want your only son to become a small part of a huge, dehumanized, computerized educational process, now would you?

That's what college is all about, or so I am told.

So frankly, I think I was much better off mooching around a variety of newsrooms, picking up what higher learning I could from editors. And while editors often try to kill their pupils, they seldom try to dehumanize them. It takes too much time.

Then there is the business of language. You always felt my lack of college education would hamper me in my chosen field.

You used to say: "Writers have to know all those big words."

Well, Mother, you certainly saved me there, even if you did so unwittingly. Any big words I did pick up came from literary critics.

If I had attended college, or so I gather from reading the college newspapers, I would have been stuck for life with a vocabulary of nothing but four-letter words.

And while many writers today are earning a handsome living using nothing but four-letter words, I would have soon found this kind of boring and looked for other work.

Such as collecting garbage.

Another point you always bring up when our conversation inevitably turns to my education gap, is that by not going to college I missed a lot of "intangibles."

These "intangibles," it would seem, involved a certain style — a way of speaking, dressing.

But please stop worrying about this, Mother. Apparently college is now a place where people communicate through a language made up of grunts, shrugs and certain key words, used on all occasions but with differing inflections, such as "man," or "wow," or "like."

But you know me and my tin ear — my inability to imitate sounds. So if I couldn't use these key words with the proper inflections I would be hopelessly inarticulate, even by college standards.

As for learning about dress — well, Mother, the kids who lived in the tar paper shacks that sprang up in Bible Hill during the Depression had a better sense of dress than that exhibited in colleges, believe me. Those kids had to wear overalls and pull-over sweaters and make-do with blankets turned into coats. But they were clean, by golly.

Another argument you always had about what I had missed by not attending some ivy-covered hall was that it would be a mind-expanding experience.

Yet all I hear from kids is that college is a "mind-destroying, soul-destroying" experience.

Surely you wouldn't have wanted to destroy your only son's soul, and what little mind he had?

When you read this, Mother, I know you will probably not agree. Old regrets die hard. And you will probably ask why, if I feel this way, I am sending my daughter to college.

So I'll tell you. It occurred to me that if college is all the kids say it is — dehumanized, computerized, mind-destroying and soul-destroying, as well as being one long drag — my daughter should find out about it.

In this way, or so I figure, if she survives, the rest of her life will be a veritable breeze, a walk in the sun.

Mind you, I am sure that many parents feel the way I do — each time they write a cheque to keep a kid in college they weep when they think of the horror to which they are subjecting their children. But they console themselves by saying: "It's for their own good."

Love,
Frank.

Jan. 13, 1970.

Just buying a car can make you a social outcast

This is the time of year when the new model automobiles come out in all their gleaming glory, and all the automobile lovers come out in a rash.

Because, complain as they will about how cars are taking over our cities or creating a pollution problem or getting too fancy, most North Americans love automobiles. And the advent of the new models is a big occasion.

These automobile lovers pour over the advertisements and take lengthy tours through the show rooms. They do this even if they aren't going to buy a new car that year — they simply love to look at cars.

All of which leaves me somewhat puzzled. Sure, I like to have a car — it gets me from point A to point B very nicely.

But aside from that, I am a big disappointment to the dedicated car salesman. I know nothing about buying a car. The last time I needed a car, in fact, I asked my wife to pick out one she liked.

When she did this, I went down to the show room on a Saturday afternoon, woke up a salesman, pointed at the model my wife had described, and said:

"I'll take that one there."

The salesman looked at me in astonishment.

"You mean you're going to buy it, just like that?"

I said that was the case.

"You mean," he queried, "you're not going to go around and kick the tires?"

182

I said I could see no sense in kicking the tires.

He blanched a bit, but tried again.

"Wouldn't you like to open one of the doors and slam it shut?" he almost pleaded. "Most car buyers simply love to slam car doors."

I explained that slamming a car door was not my idea of having a jolly Saturday afternoon.

"Well look, mister," the now almost desperate salesman said, "at least you're going to look under the hood?"

"Why should I look under the hood?" I asked.

"To look at the engine," he screamed. "Everybody has to lift up the hood and look at the engine. It's all part of the tradition of buying a new car."

I told him I didn't want to look at the engine because I didn't know anything about engines.

"All I want you to do," I said, "is tell me how much this car costs. If I can afford it, I'll take it — right now."

The salesman was a broken man. He mumbled the price. I signed a cheque. He gave me the keys.

And that was that.

Well, not exactly. A couple of months later this particular salesman bumped into my wife when she took the car back for servicing.

"That husband of yours," he said, shaking his head, "he's a real nut. He wouldn't even kick a tire for me."

Obviously, the next time I need a new car I will have to look for one at another establishment. Socially, I simply would not be acceptable at the old spot.

Sept. 19, 1970.
Weekend Magazine.

Let's leave poor Nessie alone

Frankly, I think it is time that we started to distribute LNA buttons — the LNA standing for Leave Nessie Alone.

Nessie, of course, is the nickname for the Loch Ness monster. And I, for one, believe that it is time that something was done to protect Nessie's privacy.

Mind you, I don't want any harm to come to Bill Smallfield, the Canadian who is now patrolling the banks of Loch Ness in hopes of seeing Nessie, and composing a song in her honor. But I feel that this hunt for Nessie is being overdone. As far as is known, Nessie has never harmed anybody. For centuries she has coyly hidden away in the depths of the murky Scottish loch, only occasionally popping up to give some crofter a bit of a shock, or to hypo a flagging tourist industry.

But she has never bitten anybody, carried off any children or misbehaved in any way. She is probably history's most well-behaved monster.

But lately she has been treated like some kind of criminal. People are determined to find her. Scientists have sent radar waves hurtling through the loch depths attempting to locate her home.

Some snoops even got a small submarine to help them probe the loch in hopes of finding Nessie.

Naturally, Nessie has reacted the way any lady who values her privacy would react. She has resolutely refused to make an appearance. A kind of waterloving Garbo, she remains as mysterious as ever.

What worries me is that one of these myriad searchers — privacy invaders — may some day inadvertently come across Nessie. And startled and upset, Nessie may react by biting his head off.

Then what a hue and cry there would be. There would be some who would panic and demand that Nessie's hideaway be bombed on the grounds that she was a dangerous monster.

This would be a tragedy because I feel the world can well afford to lose the occasional scientist, but it cannot afford to lose one of its few genuine monsters.

After all, how many do we have? There is the Abominable Snowman in the Himalayas, good old Ogopogo in B.C., and the Sasquatch. That is about all.

And that is why I think we have to form our Leave Nessie Alone movement right away, and get out those LNA buttons.

There is not much time left.

Jan. 24, 1970.
Weekend Magazine.

Recollections of a gunman

As a wide-eyed kid who followed the exploits of the gun-slinging desperadoes in the United States during the 1930s — the Dillingers, the Pretty Boy Floyds, the Baby Face Nelsons — in the newspapers, it never occurred to me that these people really existed.

It made for exciting reading. But to me those characters

were no more real than those upright, death-defying types I came across in the simon-pure Boys' Own Annual.

(If you don't know the Boys' Own Annual, read no further. I've just cut you off on the far side of the generation gap.)

Anyway, of all these outlaws the one who captured my fancy most was Alvin (Old Creepy) Karpis. At least it gave a red-blooded Canadian boy more goose pimples than nicknames such as Pretty Boy or Baby Face or Legs.

Old Creepy was a nickname to have nightmares by.

Or perhaps, as all this death and violence was more of a game to me than a brutal reality, it was a kid's normal desire to go with a winner.

Because, in his own lawless world, Karpis was a winner. Once, I recall, the Associated Press ran a kind of box score for hoodlums. In this were listed such luminaries as Clyde Barrow and Bonnie Parker, Dillinger, Ma Barker, Nelson and Floyd.

But the name at the top of the list was Karpis.

Frankly, I thought I had forgotten all of this until about six years ago when I heard that Karpis was still alive. In fact, there was a chance he might be paroled.

During the years that followed I kept in continual touch with Karpis. But this was not done out of any feeling of admiration — in fact, quite the reverse.

But I was curious. And also I felt that Karpis might have a worthwhile story to tell. Not a prettied-up version like the Bonnie and Clyde movie effort which turned murder and sadism into something kind of appealing.

What I wanted was a realistic, "I was there" account of what it was really like to be both the hunter and the hunted and what would make a man deliberately choose a gun as an everyday working tool.

When people hear I know the former Public Enemy Number One they ask me what he is like.

Well, today Karpis is soft-spoken, always immaculately dressed, very alert and in his quiet way enjoys the good things of life. He is an easy person to be with.

He certainly does not look back on his exploits with any pride. In fact, he says, "I was a no-good bum."

However, he seems to have no regrets.

I believe his book is the first to tell the truth about those violent days — it isn't a pretty truth, but it is fascinating.

And, after reading it I do not think any kid will be tempted to take up the calling of professional gunman. Which is all to the good.

Jan. 17, 1970.
Weekend Magazine.

In a submarine you have to know how to use your head

In the Second World War, some genius decided that we should bolster our convoy escort forces with submarines. With U-boats on the verge of winning the Battle of the Atlantic, why not send submarines to hunt submarines? Or so the theory went.

When this brilliant bit of strategy was unveiled to me, I questioned it. I mean, how did a submarine know if it was the hunter or the hunted? Would our submarines be as vulnerable as the enemy submarines?

When I asked these questions it was suggested I find out the answers — by hitching a ride in a British submarine.

So one cold, miserable February day I disappeared into the bowels of an ancient sub, a retread from the First World War.

The thing was cramped, smelled awful and water dripped from the tubular walls. The only thing that made life bearable was the crew. For no reason I could fathom, they were cheery and confident.

The first lieutenant was a Canadian. When he told me he was 19, I mentioned that this was rather young for such a rank.

He shrugged and said: "I graduated from submarine school nine months ago. Today I'm the only member of my class alive. It makes for quick promotion."

This bit of information did nothing to help *me* become cheery and confident.

When we levelled off at a running depth of about 40 feet, the skipper took pity on my obviously nervous condition. He poured me a large glass of navy rum.

After several libations, I asked to be shown to the head. For some reason this simple request filled the crew with jubilation. They not only showed me the way — everybody led the way.

The essential equipment was in a small compartment behind a steel, watertight door. Everything went well until I pushed the lever to flush the head.

At that moment a jet of icy Atlantic water came up through the head. While I watched in horror — what do they do to a reporter who has sunk one of His Majesty's submarines? — the jet continued, and the water in the compartment kept rising.

Finally I decided I either had to face total embarrassment or drown. So I opened the door.

The water flushed me out into the engine room. As I

sprawled on the floor, sodden and stupid, the crew laughed.

Naturally, I should have realized that when one is 40 feet below the surface of the ocean, a toilet does not flush normally. There is too much water pressure outside.

What I should have done was turn some valves — a fact nobody had pointed out — until I had enough pressure to more than equalize the outside pressure. Then flush.

The crew got me into dry clothes, poured me more rum and happily assured me that I had passed my initiation with flying colors.

So it worked out all right. But to this day, whenever I think of submarines, I think of how foolish I felt standing in that closet watching the Atlantic roll in.

Dec. 16, 1972.
Weekend Magazine.

Part VI

EATING AND DRINKING

or

Martinis and life's other important things

Once one of my bosses took me to lunch. The well-trained head waiter had my usual martini waiting for me as I sat down. My boss said he hoped I wouldn't mind if he didn't join me. He explained that he had a drink at lunch only when he was with somebody important.

Things like that keep happening to me . . .

The martini (I)

Now, as if to prove that the world is indeed headed for perdition at an amazing clip, we have the instant martini.

Perhaps you have already been introduced to this travesty of what once was the drinking man's best friend. You know, the pre-mix martini where, when you order your favorite tipple, a waitress gives you a toothy smile and proceeds to pour a bottle of liquid over a lonely cube of ice in a glass.

Or, worse still, there is the instant, portable martini. This is a liquid carried in a plastic envelope, the theory being that when one wants a drink one reaches into a pocket, extracts a plastic envelope and gulps down the contents.

Kind of like taking a shot of medicine at a prescribed time.

Now, I am not against progress. Some time ago I came up with the 24-hour martini.

This calls for a 40-ounce bottle of your favorite gin. From this bottle you extract three ounces of gin, which you drink immediately.

Then you replace the three ounces of missing gin with three ounces of good, dry vermouth. Then, after tilting the bottle gently a few times — one never shakes the bottle because, as everybody knows, gin bruises easily — you place the bottle in the freezing compartment of your refrigerator for a minimum of 24 hours.

After this ageing process, one takes a chilled glass and pours in the ice-cold mixture. One good thing about this is that it eliminates the use of ice when making a martini.

Ice, as we all know, has a tendency to melt. So, while that first martini may be cold and very dry, the second one is apt to be cold — and somewhat wet.

And a wet martini — well, one might as well eat a soggy piece of cake.

However, it seems that the newer, or younger, set of martini drinkers do not take their calling seriously. The other day, for instance, I was invited into a home for a martini.

My host poured some fluid out of a jug and handed it to me. I took a sip — and immediately began to get the feeling as though the fillings in my teeth were coming loose.

"Great stuff," my young friend commented. "Pre-mixed. No fuss, no bother."

"No martini, either," I muttered. But instead of getting angry I decided to give him some of the benefit of my experience.

I went out to my car where, by sheer coincidence, there was a bottle of top-notch gin. There wasn't time to prepare, for his delight and amazement, my 24-hour special, but I did make do as best I could.

"First," I said, pouring his version of a martini down the sink, "you fill up a nice fat jug with ice.

"Then you take the juice of one bottle of gin and pour it over the ice cubes — like so — until the jug is comfortably full. Nothing makes a martini drinker more nervous that a half-empty jug.

"You let it chill, or age, for approximately two minutes and then you pour, and drink."

My young friend did as he was told. He poured and drank. He then poured and drank again.

A short while later, as I was continuing to admire my handiwork, I noticed my young friend was no longer with me.

Some time later his wife told my wife that my young

friend had quietly gone up to his room and stayed in bed for three days. My wife also reported that my young friend's wife had not sounded too pleased about the whole thing.

You know how it is, some wives can't abide having their husbands enjoy a good, three-day sleep.

But then, as my wife was berating me for leading my young friend astray, it struck me that I had made one mistake. When I was demonstrating how a real, old-fashioned martini should be mixed, I had made one small error.

While I was pouring the gin over the ice, the vermouth bottle, with the cap off, was standing a good six inches from the jug. And everybody knows it should stand about three inches from the jug.

The martini was just a mite too dry, that's all.

April 25, 1970.

The martini (II)

Of late, there have been a few of my readers writing to suggest that my ill-disguised liking for the occasional martini is somewhat reprehensible. And for a few weeks I felt pretty badly about this, let me tell you.

But then another reader came to my aid. He sent me a two-year-old issue of Gourmet magazine containing an article eulogizing the (you guessed it) martini. I felt so good about this I thought I would pass along some of the information I picked up while reading this article — information I am sure fellow-martini addicts will appreciate.

(Non-martini addicts at this point are advised to turn to

the section of this newspaper which tells us all how marijuana is less damaging to one's virtue and liver than gin.)

The Gourmet article was written by J. A. Maxtone Graham, and this is the lead:

"Who can visualize the world before 1860, a world in which the dry martini had no place? It must have been a bleak and arid earth that lacked the frosty, limpid, and luminous brew that today transforms the weary, work-laden executive into a sparkling and rejuvenated companion, or makes the child-bound housewife feel, for one evening hour, like a queen."

The article was of great reassurance to me because it told of other writers who were martini addicts. In fact, the article said, back in 1949 the late Bernard De Voto, in Harper's, described the martini hour in these words:

"This is the violet hour, the hour of hush and wonder, where the affections glow again and valor is reborn, when the shadows deepen along the edge of the forest and we believe that, if we watch carefuly, at any moment we may see the unicorn."

Naturally, the article delves into those never-ending arguments as to what makes up the perfect martini, and how it should be mixed. But no rigid or non-negotiable stand is taken.

The writer, like all martini drinkers, is a cultivated, easy-going person and he admits that while the arguments do exist, they really do nothing more than add to the enjoyment of martini drinking.

He says, for instance, that survival kits should all contain a quantity of gin, a smidgin of vermouth, and a small mixing vessel.

Then, if lost, a man should start to mix his martini. Immediately, claims the writer, a friendly and helpful native would appear as if by magic, tap our lost soul on the shoulder and tell him scornfully:

"That's a hell of a way to fix a martini."

The martini, our writer claims, can not only be used as a sure-fire rescue tool for intrepid explorers. It is also one of the great inducements to peace we now have — and in our violence-torn world this should not be overlooked.

To prove his point he tells of an incident in Stockton, California. There a group of ladies were at the peak of their martini happiness when two armed burglars broke in and announced at gunpoint that they wanted the ladies' jewelry and money.

Instead of the usual panic and violence, the partying ladies merely smiled sweetly and asked the intruders to join them for a drink. Baffled by the whole affair, the burglars left empty-handed, and the party continued unabated.

Ah, peace, it is wonderful.

The article also pointed out that as far as could be ascertained the world's largest martini is served in a Minneapolis restaurant. This restaurant sells a six-gallon martini for $195.

But the restaurant will sell only one to a customer. So don't all of you start heading for the Nirvana that is known as Minneapolis.

Anyway, that is my defence of the martini. And if I stick to my guns, or glasses, I may, as Bernard De Voto suggests, be lucky enough someday to see the unicorn.

May 28, 1970.

When summers were worth living

The other day, as I watched a flock of kids romp out of a school to signify that school was over for another year and summer was officially here, I began to wonder if there were any old-fashioned grandmothers around today to help make summer the memorable experience it should be.

I mean, today grandmothers seem hard to find. I am sure they exist, but they are not easily recognizable.

They are stylishly slim, they never have grey hair and not one of them looks as though she lived in the country — and knew how to cook for a grandson.

Perhaps I am maligning grandmothers. But in my day all good grandmothers lived in the country on lovely old farms which were a delight to visit, if one was young, that is.

I was exceptionally fortunate. I had two grandmothers when I was growing up. One lived in a small village, which in the days of sail had been a bustling little port.

All day I could play around the crumbling wharfs, crawl through some of the old ships that still were there, beached in the mud and disintegrating a little more each year.

But, best of all, there was my grandmother. And her kitchen.

That kitchen was a big, sunny place perpetually filled with wonderful smells. On the top and in the oven of the huge, iron coal stove there were always several things baking, boiling, stewing, roasting or steaming.

A fellow got more nourishment out of taking a couple of deep breaths in that kitchen than he can now from eating an entire, modern meal.

This particular grandmother was convinced that all growing boys were perpetually on the verge of starvation and that pie was the answer to all problems.

She was, in fact, one of the most sensible women I have ever met. And when she baked a lemon pie, well, the only polite thing a grandson could do to show his appreciation was to ask for seconds, and even thirds.

My other grandmother lived on a small farm. Out front was an orchard and in the early morning when the rising sun was burning off the mist, you could sit quietly on the front porch and watch the deer come out of the nearby forest to breakfast on apples.

Nobody ever bothered the deer. Heck, there were enough apples for them and for us, too.

Then, after the mist had completely cleared, my grandmother and I would go out and pick the mushrooms that had popped up overnight. So our breakfast would be mushrooms, fried in home-made butter, on toast, made from home-made bread.

If you can think of a better way to start the day, from an eating standpoint, I would like to hear about it.

Naturally, every old-fashioned grandmother realized that a growing grandson needed a snack prior to going to bed.

So in the cool of the evening, in the proper season, we would go out and pick a pail of blueberries. Then, back in the kitchen, I would fill a big porridge bowl with the fresh-picked berries and drown them in thick Jersey cream, supplied that very evening by our very own Jersey cow.

That's the way it used to be. Perhaps, in some places, it still is. But I have a hunch, now that we have become mainly an urban nation, that for the most part today's grandmothers live in city apartments and, to compound the

199

horror, are just as careful about calories and balanced diets and the rules of nutrition as any ordinary mother.

More's the pity.

June 27, 1970.

A simple song of thanksgiving

Now that this is "Be Nice To China" time, everybody is busily trotting out stories to prove the Chinese really are nice.

So, as I am not one to stand in the way of a bandwagon, I would like to add my Oriental version of the two cents' worth.

My theory is that without the Chinese an awful lot of Canadians would either have starved, or died of ptomaine poisoning.

Today's Canadians do not know this. They travel from spot to spot and find clean, comfortable and safe eating places from coast to coast. One can even face up to a meal in Toronto.

But I would like to remind these people that this was not always so.

Just a few decades ago eating in Canada was to play a gastronomic version of Russian roulette. With the exception of Montreal — "Once you leave Montreal, you are camping out" — a fellow in a strange town literally took his life in his hands when he tried to decide where he should eat.

That is, he took his life in his hands unless he travelled under Lowe's First Rule For Survival On The Road. LFRFSOTR was this:

When in doubt, look for the nearest Chinese restaurant.

In those dim and almost forgotten days of 20 to 25 years ago, Canada for the most part was a culinary disaster area. As a reporter who was then constantly on the road I did not frighten myself with the thought of being fired.

My worries were of a more immediate concrete nature. For instance, would I die of starvation or food poisoning? As I said, today things are infinitely better.

But then, when lured by duty to a small prairie community or a mining town in northern Ontario, there was only one solution to the eating problem.

That solution was to find the nearest Chinese restaurant.

Sure, sure — I know all the jokes and stories about Chinese restaurants. But I also know that without them I, and thousands of other wanderers, would not have survived.

A Chinese restaurant, first of all, was clean. It smelled good when you went in. It might be a small place in a small town and it was probably called The Maple Leaf Cafe — but it was good and it was cheap.

In such places a stranger was also safe. The waiters were polite and the management did not let large surly types hang around.

Mind you, there was the business of monotony. Once, on the trail of a disaster story, I had to spend quite a few days in a mining town.

Eating three meals a day in the one Chinese restaurant extant became a bit of a drag. Or so I thought until the morning I decided to have breakfast in the hotel where I had a room.

Cold eggs swimming in cold grease, with a couple of pieces of limp bacon garnishing the side of the plate, are not my idea of Nirvana in the morning. So at lunch that day I was back in the Maple Leaf Cafe — being bored, I figured, was a hell of a lot better than being a hospital patient.

What amazed me was how the Chinese knew where to place their restaurants. Most Canadians wait until there is a gold strike or an oil strike to move to the scene of action.

But as far as I could figure out, a resourceful Chinese chef would first build his restaurant. Then somebody would wander into the neighborhood and find gold, or oil.

Could it be that once a prospector saw a Chinese restaurant he knew there simply had to be riches in that area?

Anyway, I felt that as we are now on a Love China kick, I would sing my simple song of thanksgiving. Name practically any town or hamlet in Canada, and I can tell you about the menu in the Chinese restaurant there.

And I am very grateful to be able to do so — otherwise I would be in an advanced state of malnutrition.

Mar. 7, 1972.

Breakfast can be beautiful

Sometimes it seems to me that the best meal of all is breakfast. Not any old breakfast — but a breakfast on a lazy Sunday morning after the family has cleared out of the kitchen and I am alone with the refrigerator and the stove.

One of the finest parts of such a morning is the anticipation. I can lie in bed waiting for the kitchen to clear of its female traffic and start the day by remembering some great breakfasts of the past.

There was the time when I was a believer in having the main part of breakfast made up of kippered herring and scrambled eggs. But eventually my wife, who has a very sensitive nose, put her foot down and it has been a long time since I have hotted up a kipper on a Sunday morn.

Then there was the time I breakfasted on wild strawberries, thick cream and champagne — but what the heck, that kind of thing is out of the question with prices the way they are now. But it is kind of nice to remember; it was cool and simply delicious.

So, after running through the breakfasts that have been, I try to concentrate on the breakfast that is to be. Mentally I catalogue what might be in the refrigerator.

A couple of nights ago we had some delicious home-baked beans, so there is bound to be at least one small container of left-over beans. No one else in the house will eat left-over beans, but I happen to think they are yummy.

Eggs present no problem, except what form to have them in. Of late I find my scrambled eggs are not as dry and fluffy as they should be, so perhaps I should try again.

Bacon, these days, is always a headache. The strips the packing houses put out — thin and almost meatless strings put up in bright red packages so the buyer thinks he is really getting something he can get his teeth into — are hardly worth putting in a pan. By the time they are ready to eat they are wizened little bits which will hardly fill a tooth cavity.

But perhaps, just perhaps, my wife will have remembered to order some of that back bacon I like so much. Or visited a certain store where the bacon is cut to specifications. If that happened, well, life will be worth living.

Wait a minute? Did I remember to tell my wife about those sausages I wanted? Or did I forget? A Sunday morn-

203

ing breakfast without a fat and succulent sausage or two is no breakfast at all. Well, this adds an element of suspense to the enterprise.

Another suspenseful element is the coffee. My wife quite often orders instant coffee, not because she enjoys drinking it but because she thinks it helps her diet. And there have been Sunday mornings when I have created the almost perfect breakfast only to face up to the fact that there is nothing but instant coffee in the house.

Then, just as I am getting really worried, a delectable fragrance drifts up the stairs from the kitchen. That is real coffee that is perking down there, so now all I have to do when my turn at the kitchen comes is to throw out the coffee my wife has brewed (she likes it thin) and prepare my own dark and tangy drink.

Yes, those Sunday breakfasts are great. And one of the nicest things about them is that if I am lucky, and the family goes out on one of those mysterious Sunday errands, I can finish eating and then tip-toe back upstairs to get a really good nap on a full stomach.

Sometimes life can be wonderful.

Nov. 23, 1965.

Dazzling menu for corn lovers

The man on the phone said he was calling because the new corn was coming in and, as he knew I was a corn fancier, he would like to know how long one should boil new cobs of corn.

"No more than eight to 10 minutes," I said, "and boil them reverently."

'That's what I thought," my caller said. "But my wife insists on boiling corn for about 40 minutes. Is there anything I can do about this?"

Fresh, newly-picked corn on the cob, being boiled for 40 minutes. The horror of it. So all I could tell my caller was:

"Well, you could always sue for divorce."

To non-corn addicts this may sound harsh. But for those of us who know the true deliciousness of new corn, eaten no more than 15 to 20 minutes after it is picked, such a solution sounds logical.

At this point I realize there are some corn lovers who already are reading this with a curl of the lip. That bit about eating corn "20 minutes after it is picked" will do it.

Such people are the true corn fanatics. They are such purists they insist that the only corn worth eating has to be grown in your own back yard. And the back yard must slant down towards the back door so after the corn is picked a fellow can shuck it as he runs down hill towards the house where the pot of water is already boiling on the stove.

That way the corn is only 10 minutes old when it is finally eaten. Any corn older than that, these people insist, is not fit for human consumption.

However, I am a little more lenient than that. We can't all have a back yard full of corn — most of us these days have to go and look for corn when the news spreads that it is ripe.

But there are limits. There is, for instance, a man I know who does grow corn in his garden at the back of his house.

"That's the only reason I have a house," he explains with the simplicity of the born corn-lover. "So a couple of times a year I can eat corn the way it should be eaten."

Anyway, one day last year he cut all the ripe cobs and found that he had too many for his family. So he generously loped over to a neighbor's and offered the woman of the house the extra ears.

'Thank you so much," the woman said. "Tonight we're having another vegetable, but I'll put these ears in the freezer and we'll have them later."

"The hell you will," my friend said rudely, grabbing back his proffered gift. "Anybody who would treat corn like that doesn't deserve any."

Mind you, to live up to these standards takes a little planning and work. But the true corn-lover accepts this cheerfully.

I recall, for instance, the summer in P.E.I. when the lobster season on our coast coincided with the ripening of the first new corn. The prospect of having fresh lobster *and* fresh corn was so delightful I nearly became unhinged, but did hold on to enough of my faculties to plan my day like this:

First thing in the morning I made a quick drive to Charlottetown. There I picked my own lobsters off the boats and waited while they were boiled on the wharf. Then it was back to the cottage to pop the lobsters into the fridge — I like my boiled lobsters cold.

Then came a visit to the lovely lady who made all kinds of home-made goodies to tell her what I needed that evening, and precisely when I would be calling.

About 6 p.m., after a couple of my own home-made, deep-dish martinis, I roared out to a nearby cornfield and cut the ears.

Back to the cottage where the water was already boiling in the pot. This gave me eight to 10 minutes to visit the cooking lady and pick up the home-made bread (hot out of the oven), the home-made blueberry pie (hot out of the oven), and the home-made ice cream.

Then it was back to the cottage for fresh, cold boiled lobster dipped in melted (home-made) butter, accompanied by 10-minute-old corn dripping with butter, and the hot bread used to generally mop up. This was followed by the home-made blueberry pie with the home-made ice cream on the top and dripping down the sides.

As I said, it took a little planning. But as every corn-lover will agree, it was worth it.

Aug. 26, 1969.

Tummies get old, too

It was in Philadelphia, I believe, when I first realized that the cast iron, nickel-plated stomach of my youth had developed a few rust spots.

I was hitching a ride in a United States Air Force plane — a rather decrepit DC-4 with built-in draughts — from Colorado Springs to New Mexico when, for a reason known only to the plane, we fluttered down out of a snowy sky and limped into an air field near Philly.

As the pilot admitted he had no idea how long it would take to get our aged iron bird back on the wing, I moved into a Philadelphia hotel to await the results of the emergency operation.

The following day, about noon, I got up and discovered that across the street from the hotel was a fabulous smoked meat emporium.

As I am a smoked meat addict, I immediately crossed the street. It was heaven. There were more than 40 varieties of smoked meat available so I had a plate of my favorite kind, with some potato salad and a side order of home-baked beans. All this was washed down with a few flagons of delicious German beer.

Man, that's some breakfast, let me tell you.

A few hours later the phone rang and the pilot told me we were about to attempt to get our DC-4 airborne. And that evening, while tossing about in some turbulence, it occurred to me that my stomach was growing old.

That attack of indigestion must have lasted a week.

Anyway, I swore off smoked meat. As much as I loved it, the taste simply wasn't worth the price.

That was several years ago. But then, last night, I suffered a sudden attack of hunger pangs just as I was walking past this city's best smoked meat emporium.

I stood there, nose pressed against the glass, and watched as all those lucky people chomped away on that delicious smoked meat.

The next thing I knew, I was in that emporium. I told myself that I would have only one smoked meat sandwich. One smoked meat sandwich would not harm me.

So when the waiter came I said firmly:

"Two smoked meat sandwiches, please. Make them medium."

Surely two sandwiches would be all right. And I had ordered the medium brand, hadn't I?

I had — and I must say they were delicious. After my abstinence, they tasted even better than I had remembered. I was very careful, too. No side dishes. My beverage was healthful milk.

I walked out feeling great. My euphoria was such that I planned a future whereby, if I exercised due care and restraint, I could occasionally indulge myself with a smoked meat sandwich.

That was about 10 p.m. At 3 a.m. I shrieked: "Turn the plane back to Philadelphia — I'm dying."

My wife shook me fully awake and assured me I wasn't in a plane and that I was nowhere near Philadelphia.

"Well," I said, clutching my aching tum, "it feels like Philadelphia.

So today all I can say is that if you think it is any fun trying to write a column while doubled over in agony — well, you're welcome to try.

Aug. 28, 1971.

Yo, ho, ho, and kindred demons

It occurred to me last Sunday, àpropos of nothing, that 30 years ago on that date I had become the unofficial rum drinking champion of the British Commonwealth.

I stress the "unofficial" part of it because the man who taught me this fine art, and who is definitely my superior, is still alive and might read this.

Anyway, the whole thing occurred because I was kidnapped. I was supposed to sail from Londonderry to Newfoundland in a Canadian corvette. The night prior to sailing there was a party.

The next morning I found I was aboard a corvette all right, but everybody was talking kind of funny. I considered this for some time as I watched the placid surface of the Foyle River slide by but really didn't solve the mystery until that noon.

At that magic moment the skipper announced pinkers would be served — the last drink any of us would have until we hit Newfoundland. Pinkers, I might explain, is the only drink I know which is more lethal than a dry martini.

So in the goodwill generated I managed to get my courage up to the point where I could ask what ship I might be in.

It was a Royal Navy corvette, which accounted for the funny talk. But how had I, a Canadian war correspondent, gotten aboard a British ship?

The captain's explanation was beautifully simple. At the height of the party the previous night the officers of the British corvette decided they were being snubbed because no war correspondents had ever sailed with them. The British correspondents always chose to sail with the battle-wagons and destroyers — more class.

So, as a point of pride, they decided to abduct me. After this logical explanation the skipper looked at his 21-year-old captive and added.

"You don't look like much of a war correspondent, but then we aren't much of a ship."

In this amiable spirit we plodded along the familiar "north of 50" convoy route and about three weeks later were tied up in Argentia, Newfoundland.

Argentia, in those early days of the war, was not a sailors' delight. There was no place to go and nothing to do. So we had to devise our own amusements.

Which is how the rum drinking tournament came about.

There were men from all parts of the Commonwealth in that little fleet. So the evening after we had tied up, a group from our corvette hippety-hopped from ship to ship until we got to an Australian corvette.

There my skipper informed me I had been chosen to defend the honor of his ship in the rum drinking joust.

The ship, he solemnly warned me, had 50 quid riding on me so unless I wanted to swim to Halifax . . .

The contest began. After the pace had been established and things were moving along, it seemed to me that my main opponent would be the skipper of the Australian corvette.

He was a big man, immaculately dressed in old flannels, a white turtle neck sweater, a great curly beard and a gold earring in the lobe of his right ear.

But I was mistaken. As we came into the home stretch he sighed deeply, put his head down on the wardroom table and went to sleep.

The dark horse was a slim, shy South African sub-lieutenant about my age. That boy had class. The elbow bent smoothly, the Adam's apple bobbed easily and there was no vulgar lip-smacking.

In fact, he had so much class I began to worry. I loved swimming in those days, but not in those waters.

Perhaps the thought of the icy fate awaiting me if I failed was what did it. Because, about half an hour after the Aussie had folded, the South African slid quietly out of his chair.

There I was, the unofficial rum drinking champion of the British Commonwealth. And my reward was half the money won, plus all the free rum I wanted.

I am not greedy, so I acepted the money and turned down the rum.

Aug. 8, 1972.

And all because of an aching back

F rankly, despite what other people may say, I think I am handling the unexpected problem of sobriety fairly well.

It all came about because of my back. It had been acting up. Finally, when I needed assistance to climb out of bed, my wife insisted I see a doctor.

Now, I have nothing against doctors. In fact, I didn't complain even when my sister married one, which shows how broad-minded I am.

Anyway, I took my aching back to my doctor. He struck me a sharp blow on the spine and didn't have to say, "Does that hurt?"

Instead, he ordered me to stop screaming — "Think of the patients out in the waiting room," he said crossly.

Finally he decided that before he could tell what had happened to my back he had to get the muscles relaxed. To do this he ordered me to take some pills.

That seemed like an easy out to me, so I thanked him and prepared to leave. Then he dropped the hammer.

"Of course," he said, "you won't be able to take a drink when you're taking the pills. If you do, you'll get a bad reaction."

However, I straightened my shoulders — and immediately shrieked in agony again — and prepared to face the future, as dry and grim as it might be.

The first morning didn't bother me at all. But then came lunch. I hobbled to the door — that back of mine causes me to walk in a somewhat peculiar manner — headed for my favorite lunchtime spa.

"Here's your lunch," my secretary said, stopping me in my tracks.

I looked. In front of me was a toasted, fried egg sandwich and a container of lukewarm, brown fluid alleged to be coffee.

I walked around this apparition slowly. "Lunch," I announced to my secretary, "is a delicious dry martini. Maybe two, if the company is right. Then a steak sandwich and . . ."

"Lunch," my secretary announced, "is a toasted, fried egg sandwich and coffee. If you go out to lunch, I know what will happen. So eat. Then take your pill."

Somehow, a pill is not an adequate substitute for a dry martini.

The real test came a few days later. I arrived home in the evening and my wife asked:

"What's the matter, the club burn down?"

"Very funny," I said.

Then I looked at her right hand. In it was clutched a pre-dinner drink.

But I controlled myself nobly. I didn't shout or scream or tell her, "When I don't drink, nobody drinks." I merely hobbled to my easy chair, now buttressed with pillows, and had a hot cup of tea.

How's that for high living in the suburbs?

But then came dinner. My wife had acquired some lovely lobsters from a Maritime friend and we were having them cold.

My eyes and stomach lit up. I flew to the cold kitchen and snaffled onto a bottle of white wine. I hummed as I opened it.

But as I poured I noticed there were only two glasses. "One for me and one for my mother," my wife said.

"You can have your pill."

Have you ever washed down cold lobster with ice water? Flavored with the salt from your own tears?

As I said, however, I am handling the problem very well. No tantrums, no complaints. I mean, not drinking is no problem at all, really. Not for me.

My wife helps me, too. She claims I am losing weight.

"You will look much better," she tells me, "once you can walk again so people can see your face."

There is a light — a very small one, but a light — at the end of the long, dry tunnel.

Dec. 4, 1969.

Home-made ice cream (I)

Now that ice cream weather has finally arrived, the lovers of that cool, smooth delicacy are busily recalling — between enjoyable slurps — great moments in ice cream.

Some say the world's best ice cream is found in Naples. Others, after a quick glance around to make sure there is no RCMP member nearby, are sure that Cuba's brand is the best.

But somehow I can't get in on this name-dropping, globe-skipping ritual. Because I know that nobody will believe me if I tell them that the world's best ice cream was once made by a fellow called Bill Robbins.

He made it in a woodshed in Bible Hill.

Bill was probably the best friend my family ever had.

A big, handsome Irishman, he was road construction boss by trade. But he loved to cook. And if he remembered to put at least half the wine in the food, and only half in himself, he could produce some masterpieces.

But Bill, as far as my friends and I were concerned, really achieved true greatness in the summer. Often, on a hot Sunday afternoon, we would return from Sunday school to find Bill out in the woodshed.

On the floor would be a large burlap bag holding a cake of ice and Bill would be busy reducing this single cake to hundreds of chunks, using the blunt end of an axe.

Then we knew that soon there would be great mounds of smooth, cool, delicious home-made ice cream.

The one thing we didn't know was what flavor it would be. Bill would have the stuff already mixed and hidden in the metal compartment of the wooden freezer before we got there. But, as all of his concoctions were equally delicious, we didn't mind that. In fact, the suspense gave the alfresco, woodshed party a bit of a fillip.

After the ice had been properly crushed, it and the rock salt would be piled in the wooden bucket around the metal container.

Then my friends and I would take turns at the crank. It was a contest to see who could turn it the longest but finally the moment came when the crank would not move another inch.

At which point, as we watched wide-eyed, Bill would flex his muscles, hold the freezer with his left hand and then, with his mighty right hand, easily give the crank another half-dozen or more turns.

After that the ice cream was officially ready. Not just a

215

cone of ice cream or a plate of ice cream — a whole freezer of ice cream.

We didn't have to worry about spoiling our appetites because in those days everybody had their big meal at noon. On Sunday it would be roast beef or chicken, with supper a less formal affair with cold meat or chicken.

And who needed to save an appetite for cold cuts?

So when Bill took the top off the freezer we would be poised, big spoons at the ready, to see what we were to have. I used to say a small prayer in favor of strawberry, but I really wasn't too disappointed if it was peach or vanilla or raspberry.

I mean, who cares which road he takes as long as heaven is the final destination?

So, with all due respect to those who have a thing about ice cream in Naples or ice cream in Cuba, I still maintain that the very best ever produced was produced in a woodshed in Bible Hill.

As far as I can remember, all the years this sub rosa ice cream emporium operated, there was only one failure. And it wasn't an ice cream failure.

It was a case of outside interference.

One Sunday afternoon just as we began our innocent orgy my grandmother happened by. She remarked on how good the ice cream looked so, as a well mannered boy, I offered her a lick from my spoon.

She licked — and then screamed to my mother in the house: "He's feeding these children rum. On a Sunday at that."

Bill's desire to innovate had gotten the better of him and that was one ice cream crop we lost.

June 20, 1972.

Home-made ice cream (II)

Remember the joys of home-made ice cream?

Well, maybe you don't. Perhaps you are not old enough, or perhaps you didn't have the advantage of being brought up in a small town.

Because long after the cities were inundated with store-bought ice cream, the home-made variety was still flourishing in the small towns and in the country.

Every home, or so it seemed to me, had its wooden bucket, the metal container and the handle for churning. And during those long, lazy and warm days of July and August, when kids had nothing to do but swim and run and help bring in the hay, it was ice cream eating time.

And what ice cream it was.

First, one used real thick, yellow jersey cream. Then one added fresh fruit, picked that very day.

After that came a little muscle work to whet the appetite. Ice and salt had to be packed into the wooden bucket around the metal container, and then a small boy could churn away until the mixture got so stiff the handle would no longer turn.

At that precise moment the ice cream was ready.

My favorite, if one can pick a favorite under such circumstances, was strawberry ice cream.

Once a year, I recall, the ladies of the church in New Annan, N.S., had a Strawberry Festival. There were all kinds of pies and cakes with strawberry base.

But best of all there were gallons and gallons of home-made ice cream. And you haven't lived until you have had strawberry shortcake (made of home-made shortcake and packed with fresh-picked berries) smothered in home-made strawberry ice cream.

It even beat Blueberry Grunt — and don't tell me you've never eaten Blueberry Grunt.

Anyway, that was the festival. It was held in a grove of trees with a river for skinny-dipping far enough away so the good ladies of the church would not be disturbed — but not so far that we couldn't keep tabs on how the preparations were coming along.

After all, nobody wanted to be late when the goodies were finally laid out.

Knowing the fickleness of Nova Scotia weather, I realize this can't be true. But I can never recall it raining on Festival day. The sun was always shining .

The only slightly unhappy experience I can recall was when, along with an equally greedy friend, I snitched a whole container of ice cream.

Then the two of us went to a secluded spot with our spoons and ate and ate and ate. Then we ate, albeit slowly, some more.

Why we went to the trouble of stealing the ice cream I can't recall because for 25 cents one could eat as much of anything or everything one could hold.

But steal the container I did. And that night I swore off ice cream — and held to my vow for almost two days.

July 17, 1971.
Weekend Magazine.

A taste of the past

It is nice to know that one of my favorite arguments, despite what my opponents say, is not completely made up of equal parts of nostalgia, memory and age.

What I am talking about is food.

For some time now I have been arguing that things like the apples and vegetables I ate in my youth tasted better than those same products taste today.

Nonesense, said my opponents. I thought this way because of a sense of nostalgia and also because memory has a way of playing tricks on us — making the past a little rosier than it really was.

They also said — and this was the unkindest remark of all — that as I grew older my taste buds deteriorated, so naturally things didn't taste as good as they once did.

But then along came the natural food boom and suddenly I realized that I had been right all along.

I was completely convinced of this when I read about the farmers, the very few farmers, who now are growing foods naturally — no pesticides, no chemicals.

You see, I had a stepgrandfather who did just this. Not that he knew he was doing it — he did it because it was easier that way.

At about age 45, as close as I can figure, he took a look at the 1910 rat race, sensibly said the hell with it, and retired to a farm.

The farm had a big apple orchard, a vegetable garden and all kinds of fruit trees. And to my knowledge he never did a thing to help those vegetables and fruits grow.

They were on their own.

Well, quite often, in the cool of a summer evening when he was in the right mood, he might sit out on his front porch and sing to them. At least, I assumed he must be singing to them because nobody else was around — at such times my grandmother barricaded herself in the house and refused to sit out on the front porch.

But he certainly had no intention of spraying his crops with insecticide or pumping the earth full of chemicals designed to aid growth. In the mornings he would be up at dawn and the two of us would walk around the farm, pausing here and there to pick mushrooms.

Then we would retire to the kitchen where we would have a breakfast of mushrooms and bacon. Delicious.

Dinners, I recall, were superb. The vegetables which — depending on your point of view — had survived, or thrived on his rather peculiar approach, had a flavor you can hardly imagine.

And, for desert, have you ever had blueberries, picked in your back pasture, still warm with the sun and covered with thick cream from your own Jersey cow?

That's natural food for you, by golly. And proof that age and my deteriorating taste buds (what a frightful thought!) are not the reason things tasted better then — even the apples, the ones which had survived the bugs and slugs, and deer which ventured out in the morning mist to feast in the orchard, were juicier and sweeter.

Mainly because my stepgrandfather, without even knowing it, was growing foods the natural way. It seems a shame that while today he would be praised for this, in his time he was considered a bit of a nut.

Jan. 9, 1971.
Weekend Magazine.

What is more cultural than home-made pie?

It struck me as I was reading an article on Canada's new feminists that if this sort of thing continues and grows the life of a small boy in this country is going to be pure hell.

No, I'm not worried about the big boys, the adult males, who will have to adjust to the "new woman." That will be their problem, thank goodness.

But can't help thinking of the legions of little boys who, if all women go the militant route and desert the home, will not be able to indulge in my favorite childhood sport — living off the land.

The sport used to be mainly a Saturday morning event. After breakfast I would set out. I would walk clear across town, all the way to Smith Avenue, because this was a jaunt that gave my breakfast a chance to settle.

First stop would be at the home of Mrs. Miller. She made the biggest, the crispest gingersnaps in town. By coincidence, she always made a batch on Saturday morning.

If my timing was right, Mrs. Miller would be pulling the last batch of gingersnaps out of the oven just as I arrived. So what could be more natural than for her to offer me some, and sit with me on the back porch while I washed them down with a glass of cold milk?

Then I would start to work my way back towards home. There would be a stop to check on Mrs. Roby to make sure her weekly chocolate cake was up to par. And the only neighborly thing to do was to pause for a chat with Mrs.

Matthews — particularly when it was a well-known fact that Mrs. Matthews was the best apple pie producer in the entire area.

Not each Saturday morning was the same. Some days, for instance, my nose would tell me as I strolled along that Mrs. MacKenzie was having one of her irregular, but delicious, home-made bread-making sprees.

A visit would net a friendly boy a piping hot slice of home-made bread right out of the oven, home-made butter dripping off the edges — and the whole thing drowned in dark brown molasses. I used to wish that Mrs. MacKenzie was more a creature of habit than she was, but one can't expect everything.

Then there was Mrs. Johnson (cinnamon rolls), Mrs. Rockwell (shortcakes) and Mrs. Henderson (home-made strawberry ice cream, wow!) to crowd in before it was time to head home for lunch.

And I always looked forward to lunch, because on Saturday it featured raisin pie. My mother, incidentally, was the world's best baker of raisin pie.

Anyway, that's how it went on a lazy, sunny Saturday back before the days of the new feminists. But it is a time little boys — if the article is right — may never know again.

Because if the new feminists have their way, the kitchen will be deserted in the years to come. No self-respecting woman will be caught dead in such a degrading milieu. They'll all be out doing things they consider cultural, meaningful and important.

But all I can ask is what is more cultural, meaningful and important than a beautiful home-made pie, particularly for a small boy?

May 2, 1970.
Weekend Magazine.

The greatest put down
of all

What did yesterday's kids have to enjoy that many of today's kids don't have?

Well, for one thing, yesterday's kids had the preserving season to look forward to. Today's kids, at least a lot of them, are not so lucky.

That is why I am always happy when a food editor gets around to doing an article on the fine old art of preserving. It brings back such great memories.

It also might inspire more women, and men too, to try their hands at preserving and so keep alive a glorious tradition.

Mind you, I realize there are still many people, bless 'em, who annually put down great quantities of delicious jams and jellies and fruits and relishes.

But when I was a kid everybody did this. And each house, at this time of year, was filled with aromas which had to be sniffed to be believed.

The season, if memory serves me correctly, officially began when the house filled with the smell of fresh strawberries being simmered in large pots.

They would go into glass jars to be brought out later to chase away the winter gloom.

Then came the time for blueberries. Followed, but not necessarily in this order, by cherries and peaches and apples. Heck, if it could be grown, my mother would preserve it.

223

But the grandest aroma of all was saved for late in the fall when it came time to put down a half-ton or so of chow-chow.

Coming home from school on a crisp autumn afternoon my nose would start to twitch as I entered the yard. Chow-chow making is a hot business, so even if the weather outside was crisp, the kitchen windows would be open.

I don't know if chow-chow is really a preserve in the sense that it is made in an exact way. Each home in which I would do my youthful freeloading tackled the chow-chow problem in a slightly different manner.

Some forms would be a bit sweet. Others would be tart. As far as I could tell, each woman faced up to chow-chow time by taking every garden ingredient as yet unused, and then began to invent.

It contained vegetables and fruits, in quantities that not only varied from kitchen to kitchen but from year to year in the same kitchen.

The two constants were the hunger-provoking odors and the knowledge that when the time came to eat it, the chow-chow would be, well, you dream up your own superlative.

When we had company, I would take a modest helping of chow-chow and politely and tidily put it on the edge of my plate.

But when there was "just family", and nobody was paying too much attention, I found that the best way to eat chow-chow was with roast beef hash and mashed potatoes.

First, you mixed up the hash and the potatoes. Then you covered this with an inch or so of chow-chow. After this you thoroughly mixed everything until your plate held one great, savory mess.

It sure beats any TV dinner I've ever had.

Aug. 12, 1972.
Weekend Magazine.